# LEGENDS & LORE
## OF
# LITTLE BEAVER CREEK

# LEGENDS & LORE
## — OF —
# LITTLE BEAVER CREEK

*Michael Kishbucher*

Published by The History Press
Charleston, SC
www.historypress.com

Copyright © 2019 by Michael Kishbucher
All rights reserved

Photos by the author unless otherwise noted.

First published 2019

Manufactured in the United States

ISBN 9781467142304

Library of Congress Control Number: 2019932631

*Notice*: The information in this book is true and complete to the best of our knowledge. It is offered without guarantee on the part of the author or The History Press. The author and The History Press disclaim all liability in connection with the use of this book.

All rights reserved. No part of this book may be reproduced or transmitted in any form whatsoever without prior written permission from the publisher except in the case of brief quotations embodied in critical articles and reviews.

*For Fergie. An unassuming custodian of provincial history, he once casually advised me over a bowl of soup in a Darlington, Pennsylvania garage to be cautious when analyzing our stories, as some things are better left to the imagination. Looking back, I learned much from our far too infrequent conversations. I don't think he'd be disappointed.*

# CONTENTS

| | |
|---|---|
| Foreword | 9 |
| Preface | 13 |
| Acknowledgements | 15 |
| Introduction. Little Beaver Creek: A Wild and ~~Scenic~~ Bloody River | 17 |
| 1. Mansfield the Mythmaker | 21 |
| 2. The Pig Lady of Pennsylvania's Pioneer Era | 27 |
| 3. Esther Hale: An Ohio Ghost Town's Lady in White | 69 |
| 4. Gretchen's Lock | 80 |
| 5. The Fennell House and Other Lesser Known Little Beaver Legends | 89 |
| 6. Knobs, Frauds and the Cannelton Sun God | 105 |
| Conclusions of a Grand Experiment | 127 |
| Notes | 133 |
| Bibliography | 139 |
| About the Author | 143 |

# FOREWORD

It was a dark and stormy night.
   Not really. When asked to write a foreword explaining life with local legends, I was also asked not to use the above—the very standard of trite by Edward Bulwer-Lytton. Pfft. As if...
   No, it was actually a pleasant and balmy July dusk when our Lions Club started work on the Pig Lady Haunted Barn in Cannelton. Many members, including me, had grown up with the legend of Barbara Davidson. Cashing in on her tale by holding a haunted fundraiser in October 2010 seemed a no-brainer.
   Four years later, we closed the barn doors, having learned we were not good businessmen. Exit polls each year made it clear customers wanted something scarier than just conjuring up a centuries-old wraith. Too late we learned they were right—too much history and not enough clowns with chainsaws.
   My family is from Cannelton. My brother still lives in the house we grew up in. I could hit the Fennell House with a baseball if it took a good roll. Just beyond that landmark lay Barbara's grave and a little farther the ruins of the Vanished Village. In the other direction was the site of Fiddler's Green (a Catholic church in my youth), the weird White Cemetery (which the Lions still maintain—though we don't touch the seashells) and infamous Indian Rock.
   We grew up with the legend. To us, it was normal—we thought everyone knew about the Pig Lady. I distinctly remember at least one party

# Foreword

Century-old cemetery conch shells.

at our house where it was the topic among grownups. Dad even began asking guests as they arrived whether they had spotted her on their drive in. Everyone had a story, or at least knew someone who had had a close encounter.

Here's mine.

One night back in high school, I took an old girlfriend named Connie for a parking lesson in my El Camino. We stopped halfway up a hill on a rutted fire access road in the woods at dusk. At the top of the hill lay the ruins of the Vanished Village. At the bottom, across the main road, was Barbara Davidson's grave mouldering in scruffy woods. Perfect spot to encourage a girl to snuggle.

The road was rougher than I'd expected. My vehicle was more car than truck, and the weeds were higher than the hood. Before my headlights were out, Connie started shouting. "There's somebody out there! I see her—I SEE HER!"

"GO!" I put it in reverse—there wasn't any turning around. "GOGOGOGOGO!" she screamed, beating on me as I navigated over my shoulder downhill backward while weeds whipped over my tailgate. "SHE HAS RED EYES! SHE'S COMING! GO FASTER!"

# Foreword

I don't believe in ghosts, much less one who'd opt for a pig's head to replace her own missing one. What I did believe was that I'd be pummeled unconscious by a hysterical girl if I didn't get away from what I assumed was a classmate pranking me. That's what I told my friend Steve the next day at the school cafeteria. I'll have to admit, what he said gave me a chill.

"Yeah, but how did they know you'd be there?" he asked.

My dad, Jack, and his dad, Joe, would relish telling us kids Pig Lady stories around a backyard fire, just as my brother Greg and I told our kids. Those fireside chats kindled a flame in one of those kids, Mike, the author, my son. My son the author. I like that. Got a nice ring to it.

My son the author has used skills learned as an intelligence analyst for our military to produce this book. I hope you enjoy it as much as us local yokels who lived with these legends.

—J.M.

# PREFACE

I'm a bit of a jerk. Knowing full well most admirers of folklore will look only at the cover and maybe a book's table of contents before buying, I slapped an exquisitely mysterious image on this treatise and sucked you in. Perhaps I'm projecting, as I have stacks of tourist-targeted volumes detailing the weird from my travels coast to coast. Fair warning, this is not one of those books.

Read on if you're interested in more realistic origins of our beloved Little Beaver legends.

Remarkable and peculiar history abounds in the Little Beaver Creek region. Accounts of the northernmost point of the Confederate invasion, the wanderings of Johnny Appleseed and Charlie No-face (also known as the Green Man), the perils of the Underground Railroad and the violent death of Pretty Boy Floyd are shared widely and often in news media, web forums and anthologies across the country. Beyond these famous chronicles are several less known, but equally fascinating folktales. Unlike the more famous histories, which are rooted in fact, the stories in this study lack sufficient empirical backing. This work explores some of the unsubstantiated local legends, with the intent of either unearthing underlying verifiable roots of each or the possible motivations behind the development of urban myths.

# ACKNOWLEDGEMENTS

In the spring of 2016, I got the harebrained idea to research and write an essay both for my amusement and to try to pique the interest of volunteers for a Lion's Club clean-up project. They'd operated a Halloween attraction based on a local ghost story for several years, but it had run its course, and they needed help dismantling their prized haunted barn. I thought maybe I could show my appreciation from several states away and perhaps help scrounge up a few extra pairs of helping hands for their effort.

I'm neither an expert in folklore nor a trained historian, but I developed skills during my career that provide a unique perspective in researching these areas. I'm an experienced intelligence officer for the Department of Defense, but I was initially suspect that any would find a look at folk tales through an analytic lens entertaining. After a few flailing web posts on the Lion's Club Facebook fan site, I quickly bogged down in minutia and became frustrated. Then I managed to irritate the excellent western Pennsylvania folklorist Thomas White. Fortunately for me, this led to a few digital conversations and his offer of help.

I have a small collection of Mr. White's books. They've proved exceptionally valuable in jumpstarting my porous memory while recounting stories I learned as a youth to my children. His interest in my essay and outstanding counsel gave me the courage to continue putting pen to paper. His reassurance and conversations with a myriad of proud Ohioans and Pennsylvanians like my father, mother, wife, Paul Campbell, Wayne Bable,

## Acknowledgements

the Oswald family, Bill Bitner, Alan Ferguson, Bob and Birdie Nelson, Ray Hall and my grandparents made this possible. I hope you enjoy my version of the Little Beaver Creek legends and help to keep them as a tradition for generations to come.

INTRODUCTION
# LITTLE BEAVER CREEK

## A WILD AND ~~SCENIC~~ BLOODY RIVER

To better understand these stories, I need to begin with the valley of the Little Beaver Creek itself. It's an unassumingly beautiful, peaceful and straightforward setting spanning western Beaver County, Pennsylvania, through part of Carroll, Mahoning and southeastern Columbiana County, Ohio, finally emptying into the Ohio River. An exceptionally clean and unmolested waterway, its designation as a National Scenic River in 1974 reflects its rarity in a region long rife with industrial degradation. Many fortunate enough to call it home mistake their modest means as a problem of geography, undervaluing the valley's natural serenity. It's a depressed region, but today's economic woes are no comparison for the tribulations of the setting's violent past.

Horror and supernatural legends are either born from twisted creative imagination or kernels of truth spawning stories retold over and over, acquiring fanciful bits as time passes. Perhaps some portions of our favorite local tales are inspired by the locale's tumultuous yesteryear. The three forks of the Little Beaver just happen to lie at an important but little-known crossroads in North American history.

Running south into the Ohio River, an onramp onto this superhighway of the pre-Columbian era, the Little Beaver Valley was the backdrop of terrible events long before the stories described in this book. The seventeenth-century Beaver Wars emptied the majority of the upper Ohio River Valley's native inhabitants as they fled the well-armed Iroquois Confederacy, an ally

# INTRODUCTION

*Left*: Beaver Creek at Gretchen's Lock.

*Below*: Wild and Scenic River Marker.

# Introduction

of the Dutch and later British empires.* The mostly uninhabited territory then became a hunting ground for the Iroquois fur trading machine until the French and their native subjects began to exert dominion over it, ultimately culminating in the French and Indian War. The man primarily responsible for sparking this North American theater of the more extensive Seven Years War, a Mingo (Ohio Valley Iroquois) half-king named Tanacharison, was sought in 1753 at his hunting cabin along the Little Beaver Creek by none other than the twenty-one-year-old colonial militia officer Major George Washington.[1] First meeting at the native village of Logstown near Beaver, Pennsylvania, the half-king eventually advised the gullible Virginian to take up arms against a superior French force intent on building Fort Duquesne at the forks of the Ohio River in present-day Pittsburgh.[2] Negotiation with the French, whom Tanacharison claimed had imprisoned him as a child after boiling and eating his father, was impossible.

A skirmish at Jumonville Glen followed, during which Washington's troops captured a small French scouting unit from Fort Duquesne. The leader of the defeated force began to recite a letter from his superiors in French, a language Washington did not speak, regarding their desire to maintain peace. Tanacharison spoke French and, understanding this message might dissuade the English from further hostilities, sunk his tomahawk deep into the French ensign's skull,† eating a portion of the murdered prisoner's brains in front of Washington's stunned troops.[3] Although the war was likely imminent, this incident is widely considered to be the impetus of North American hostilities in a world conflict encompassing five continents.

After the French and Indian War, Pontiac's Rebellion, Lord Dunmore's War, the American Revolution and the Northwest Indian Wars all followed.‡ Throughout, the Ohio River remained a bloodstained no man's land of asymmetric warfare where terror was the primary weapon keeping British

---

* The Iroquois Confederacy gained control of the Ohio territory by 1656, displacing Algonquin tribes like the Shawnee and Miami, as well as Iroquoian-speaking tribes who weren't members of the confederacy like the Huron (Wyandot) and Erie.
† Ensign was the lowest-ranking commissioned officer in French infantry units until the late eighteenth century, when it became sub-lieutenant.
‡ The Seven Years War was the first global conflict, carrying over into Europe and Asia from its North American theater—known in the United States as the French and Indian War, which lasted until 1763. The British won control over French North American territories; however, France's native allies did not concede defeat, attacking and taking several British forts in Ohio and Pennsylvania in what was known as Pontiac's Rebellion in 1763. European settlement in Western Pennsylvania was not entirely safe from Indian attack until the Battle of Fallen Timbers in 1794 and it wasn't completely safe to settle in the entirety of Ohio until Tecumseh's defeat in 1813.

# Introduction

colonial and then American expansionism in check. For forty-plus years, western pioneers lived daily with the fear of a torturous death at the hands of what they perceived as savages. Tomahawking, scalping, burning at the stake and abduction of women and children were commonplace. Records show that seventeen years after the last major battle with natives in the Ohio territory at Fallen Timbers, a horseman from Hanover, Ohio, sounding a Paul Revere–like, but false, alarm panicked citizens of New Lisbon (now Lisbon) in Columbiana County. The gentleman insisted that Indians were coming, slaying and scalping all in their path at the behest of the British during the War of 1812.[4]

> *"The oldest and strongest emotion of mankind is fear, and the oldest and strongest kind of fear is fear of the unknown."*
>
> *—H.P. Lovecraft*

It's challenging to relate today to the uncertainties of pioneer life in the Ohio Valley. Relatively benign reasons to be wary of present-day wilderness include Lyme disease, rabid small mammals and the occasional copperhead snake. However, subconsciously we still go through rituals that may harken back defensive tactics ingrained in our psyche from horrible lessons learned by our forefathers. Are you comforted that your pet dog will alert against lurking danger? Do you keep a well-trimmed lawn for reasons beyond aesthetics, or does having a wide field of view surrounding your home help ease your nerves?

Beyond the previously mentioned atrocities occurring during the long Indian wars, pioneer-era woods still harbored bears, mountain lions, packs of wolves and, worse, the unknown. Americans had not yet explored much beyond the territory of the original thirteen colonies. In 1803, the year Ohio was admitted to the Union as a state, only four roads crossed the Appalachians. That same year, President Thomas Jefferson discussed with Meriwether Lewis how members of the Corps of Discovery should react if they encountered giant lions or woolly mammoths on their journey to find the Northwest Passage.[*] Even witchcraft was still real in the minds of some Americans, with the last U.S. trial not occurring until 1878.[†] Barbarity and fear leave scars. While Little Beaver legends may not have direct ties to the inhuman brutality that ravaged the region before European settlement, there were real reasons to fear dark places along the wild and scenic river.

---

[*] This mission is most commonly known today as the Lewis and Clark Expedition.
[†] In 1878, Lucretia Brown of Ipswich, Massachusetts, accused Daniel H. Spofford of being "a mesmerist, and practices the art of mesmerism…and uses his said power and art for the purposes of injuring the persons and property and social relations of others." This trial drew widespread attention for Brown's bizarre claims and for the fact that it also occurred in Salem, the site of the famous 1692 witch trials.

# 1
# MANSFIELD THE MYTHMAKER

Now that we've established the factors that may have stoked the fires of folklore in the region, it's important to look into the background of the man responsible for preserving and promoting the original legends of the Little Beaver. Without Ira Mansfield (1842–1919), many of these stories would not survive today.

Mansfield was not a particularly good writer, preferring to pen short rambling essays to accompany his favorite photos. Amateur photography, a hobby he enjoyed, was a favorite pastime of the well-off in the latter part of the nineteenth century. Mansfield's stories seem secondary to his well-staged and often odd scenes. It's these peculiar photos that first sparked my interest. My father acquired several from Rich Oswald, a former Beaver County schoolteacher who'd researched much of the folklore originating from Cannelton, Pennsylvania. Mansfield owned a summer home, cannel coal mines and an orchard here from 1870 until his passing in 1919.* He also possessed mines and a farm in nearby Negley, Ohio, a town he had a hand in developing with his partner in the railroad industry and fellow Civil War veteran General James S. Negley. Cannelton and Negley reside along two of the Little Beaver's three branches.

It's not surprising that Ira Mansfield was born from adventurous stock. He is a descendant of Major Moses Mansfield (1639–1703), for whom Mansfield, Connecticut, was named. Moses received this honor for his

---

* Cannel coal is a rare form of oil shale that burns longer than wood, leaving little ash. It is sometimes referred to as candle coal due to its clean, bright-yellow flame when ignited.

Ira Mansfield. *From* Biographical Sketches of Leading Citizens of Beaver County Pennsylvania.

*Above*: Poland, Ohio's forty-niners.

*Left*: Portion of Morgan's Surrender Tree on Display at Beaver Creek State Park.

service in King Philip's War. Ira Mansfield's great-grandfather Captain "Jack" Mansfield was personally awarded a commission in the Continental army from General George Washington for his bravery in taking a redoubt during the Battle of Yorktown.* Ira's grandfather Elkanah was a forty-niner, leaving Poland, Ohio, seeking fortune in California, but he died in route.[5] As a seven-year-old witness to his grandfather's departure, this event imprinted Mansfield's thrill-seeking spirit.[6]

Ira Mansfield enlisted to serve in the Civil War at his church in Poland, Ohio, in 1862.[7] He fought in some of the bloodiest battles of the war, was wounded and saw his regiment reduced by two-thirds over the course of the conflict.[8] Mansfield was particularly proud of one specific achievement from this part of his life. As a sergeant during a campaign in Kentucky, he captured the headquarters wagon of General John Hunt Morgan, the Confederate cavalryman who later led a terrorizing raid through Ohio that ended in Lisbon, very near Mansfield's home.[9] This bold maneuver was the farthest any Confederate force penetrated the North. Mansfield kept many items from this capture, including General Morgan's epaulets and personal Bible.[10]

Returning home from three years fighting for the 105th Ohio Volunteer Infantry, where he rose from the enlisted ranks to brevet† captain, Mansfield likely found it difficult adjusting to quiet rural life again. In 1865, he and two fellow veterans formed the first Robin Hood adventurers club, an organization he passionately promoted for the entirety of his remaining days.[11] The outdoor enthusiast group provided social networking for postwar entrepreneurs, and although never directly mentioned in his writings, the club likely provided some relief from post-traumatic stress. As or even more traumatic a problem than it is today, PTSD sufferers had very little support after the Civil War. However, Mansfield and his colleagues evidently managed the problem, then called "soldier's heart" or "irritable heart," by camping. One of Ira Mansfield's second Robin Hood Club for women members later documented this self-prescribed postwar therapy by claiming, "Enthusiasm for outdoor life is growing by leaps and bounds, and bids fare to solve the great American problem of nervous breakdowns."[12] Mansfield's later successes are a testament to his apparent tremendous fortitude.

---

\* Redoubts are fortified fighting positions made obsolete by twentieth-century maneuver warfare.
† A brevet rank is an honorary title typically given for gallantry or bravery and conferred none of the authority, precedence or pay.

Robin Hood Club travel trunk on display at the Little Beaver Historical Society Museum.

Mansfield's mines and other business ventures made him substantially wealthy, affording him time to pursue hobbies like baseball, fishing, writing, politics and becoming a pioneer in the early naturalist movement. Although not educated in botany or geology, Mansfield authored books on clay and coal deposits, as well as flora and fauna of Beaver County, Pennsylvania. He contributed extensively to the Second Pennsylvania Geological Survey by hiring two men to preserve fossils found in his mines,* of which no fewer than thirteen are named for him.[13] He was particularly interested in flowers, writing two books on the subject and preserving a wide-ranging herbarium in his home.

When his veteran friends began to pass on in later years, Mansfield reinvented the Robin Hood Club as a teachers' organization. He intended this version of the club to promote women's rights, while at the same time reinvigorating a passion for nature in the teachers and their students, whom he feared had lost interest while growing up in the midst of the Industrial

---

* His contributions to the geological survey, while important, were not the only motivation for hiring men to do this work. Mansfield profited from the sale of fossils found in his mines.

Revolution. Women from across the country, as well as locals like my great-great-grandmother, traveled to Cannelton for their annual encampments each June. The only requirement for club membership was that she taught school or was a professional and would "never ride when there is an opportunity to walk."[14]

Ira Mansfield was probably not all that interested in folklore. He spent little effort communicating details of the stories we enjoy now, as compared to his other interests. His love for camping, local history and access to a print shop as president of the Beaver Falls Tribune Printing Company almost certainly are the reasons many of our favorite local tales live on today.[15] Mansfield's retelling of ghost stories for the eager ears of Robin Hood Club members around campfires is a cherished pastime carried on to this day. However, in the late nineteenth century, this form of entertainment carried more weight. In a time before mass media, the spiritualism movement gained immense popularity as a means of nighttime entertainment.* It is unknown how much stock Mansfield attributed to the widespread phenomena that popularized séances and the use of Ouija or spirit boards, but Mansfield's books did note the incorporation of mediums and fortune-tellers in later Robin Hood encampments.[16] Whether or not Mansfield judged the spiritualism movement legitimate, his campfire ghost tales live on in one form or another today.

*The Robin campers to many swamps did speed,*
*Their paths were rugged and sore.*
*Through water lilies and beds of reeds*
*And hummocks of ferns, where the serpent feeds,*
*Not even a woman's foot ever trod before.*

—I.F. Mansfield

---

\* Spiritualism is the belief that the dead have the ability to communicate with the living through certain rituals or mediums.

# 2
# THE PIG LADY OF PENNSYLVANIA'S PIONEER ERA

My fascination with arguably the most enthralling Little Beaver legend began on a semi-clear night over thirty years ago, in a mostly forgotten Pennsylvanian border village called Cannelton. My uncle struggled to keep the corners of his mouth from turning up as he told the ghost story, drawing out as much as his broken memory could recall. My father, meanwhile, crept just beyond the campfire light. Pig squeals, as hackneyed as you'd expect, burst into the air—creating the desired effect—and I was hooked. The bizarre story about a spectral woman with a pig's head came to life once more for another impressionable mind to fearfully struggle to comprehend.

Until the Little Beaver Lions Club brought her story back to the forefront in 2010, I hadn't thought much about Barbara. My first home was a five-minute walk from the abandoned Foulks family burial ground, widely considered to be the place of her interment. Everyone here knows a version of the legend; however, facts are elusive, which inspires doubt, and I am a cynic. This flaw, or fortunate quirk, depending on your perspective, has proven prosperous, as I credit my skepticism as being the catalyst for a moderately successful twenty-one-year career in intelligence. Whereas historians deal in fact, trained analysts interpret capability, motivations and intent from details both solid and vague. Conjecture is expected and embraced in my field, which is probably why I feel less sardonic about folklore than many of the journalists and scholars who have written about Barbara before me.

Intelligence analysis is equal parts art and science. Its objective is to provide actionable information based on knowns and unknowns, but at its heart establishing one's analytic integrity is fundamental. No one blames a crisis on academic or journalistic failure, but intelligence is the knee-jerk scapegoat among politicians for a good reason. It's our job to know the enemy and provide warning. Healthy egos are necessary for academics and analysts alike, but self-recognition of biases and the avoidance of cognitive traps are central to establishing credibility in our line of work.* But then again, we never get to have fun. In this framework, I filed my first report.

## Tradecraft 101: Gather Sources

All assessments begin with a painstaking review of every detail associated with applicable theories, weighing each bit of evidence for accuracy and relevance. Typically, only primary sources exploited to present logical argumentation are revealed to intelligence consumers, and for a good reason. It is cumbersome, dry, sometimes redundant and frequently dull. For the reader's sanity, I left out much of the detail (though the editorial staff is sure this was the wrong choice).

 Rich Oswald's version of Barbara's story is most widely understood today. Under his tutelage, the story was kept alive for a time in a series of Beaver County school plays. His account contains most of the details I first learned while warming near that backyard campfire so long ago. The Lion's Club admirably resurrected the story after some neglect with Oswald's help for a charitable haunted attraction that ran for several years. Because of this, the story received the attention of renowned folklorist Thomas White in his work *Supernatural Lore of Pennsylvania.*

 In summation, Barbara McCaskey was born in South Carolina in the year following the Declaration of Independence. Siding with the rebellion, the family was driven from its property and, after the war, relocated to Pennsylvania, settling near present-day Ridge Road in Cannelton on land provided to her father, Samuel, as restitution for his loyalty to the cause. In this version, Barbara grew up on the farm tending pigs, singing and becoming a crack shot with a rifle. She was very beautiful, drawing many

---

* Cognitive traps are subconscious mental shortcuts (biases) used to make quick decisions or judgements which are often flawed.

suitors, and is eventually wooed into marriage in 1791 at the age of fifteen to an army veteran from Virginia named Nathan Davidson. They moved back to his home state, but by 1794, she had returned to her father's farm without her husband. In the summer of 1795, Barbara's entire family left for Pittsburgh to acquire goods and, upon their return, failed to locate their beloved songstress. All the neighbors took part in a thorough search, and after several days, Barbara's headless corpse was found in a crawl space beneath the family farmhouse. She is interred in a neighbor's burying ground about two miles away. Like her head, the criminal was never found. Her spectral decapitated form still allegedly haunts the fields near the north branch of Little Beaver Creek from an antique barn central to the old town to the ruins of a famed Northwest Indian War veteran's former property on the village's outskirts.

ALSO, IN 1795
*Daniel McGuiness discovers what some consider to be the most intriguing mystery in North America, the Money Pit of Oak Island, Nova Scotia.*

She sometimes appears as a disembodied face near the remnants of an ancient cannel coal mine entrance for which the town derives its name, leading some to believe her head was unceremoniously disposed of in its murky depths.[17]

The legend accompanies several modern-day encounters with her ghost. Locals documented these weird happenings on the Lion's Club's "The Pig Lady—And Other Tales of Haunted Cannelton" Facebook fan page while the Haunted Barn was still in operation. A few were brave enough to share their experiences, reprinted here with permission. These first two detail one of the more memorable experiences people had while working on the attraction in its first and second year.

It Will Frizz Your Hair, Haunted Barn promotion 2010. *Author's collection of Haunted Barn promotions.*

*Wow—Another One. After a manic four hours tonight of checking fog machines, laser lights, black lighting, strobes, rehearsals, fixing the roadside marquis, and a ton of last-minute stuff before opening night tomorrow—after all that—we had another experience.*

*Toward the end of this moonlit night, as students were almost all picked up by parents, I was torn between two minor emergencies when David, a*

*16-year-old volunteer from Wampum, came running up to me in a panic. "The field!" he yelled, "come back and look at the field!" I told him I would go down back behind the barn as soon as I could. Ten minutes later, he was still waiting there for me, transfixed on the overgrown field that will be our haunted hayride.*

*"It's gone," he said. I had brought another adult volunteer, Brian, with me. "Wow," Brian said, "I've never seen the fog do that before!" The fog usually comes in parallel to the creek and parallel to the back of the barn. Tonight, it was diagonal, a line corner to corner at a 45-degree angle, with one-half of the field covered with 3–4 feet of white fog, and the other half entirely clear. "I know," David said solemnly with his arms crossed. "It did it—I saw it."*

*David told us he had finished his duties and was watching the fog roll in when he saw "a dark pillar" rise up in the near northwest corner of the field. He described it as featureless, about 3 feet in diameter and about 6–8 feet tall. He told us it moved left and backward toward the approaching fog, that the fog then retreated from it, and then that it moved right and disappeared into the tree line. I'm not making any of this up. I'm just reporting.*

Done. *"Well, it's over…for at least a year," I sighed, driving two teenage volunteers home. "Yeah, except for…" one muttered, his sentence hanging in the air.*

*Nothing else was said. We had just finished our second year of "a grand experiment" relatively unscathed. The Pig Lady haunted barn fundraiser was behind us, for a while—one believable sighting last year and one this year. I knew what he meant and changed the subject.*

*Our local Lions Club authorized a fundraiser "haunted attraction" for the Halloween season more than two years ago. It was the brainchild of Dave O'Neill, who had befriended one Rich Oswald, school board president and historian of the Pig Lady legend, at their church. Dave had worked feverishly during the short weeks between the club's OK and the opening, only to pass away shortly before it began. He was found in his favorite chair, TV still on, after another grueling night of construction and planning at the "haunted barn." It was unexpected; he was relatively young and in good health. It was a shock. He had warned me about the Pig Lady, though.*

*The Pig Lady, Barbara Davidson—18 years old—lost her head.*

*This legend, based on fact, has persevered decades and now centuries since first recorded in local papers. And because of the "barn" project, we*

*Above*: Haunted Barn.

*Left*: Tribute to Dave. *Author's collection of Haunted Barn promotions.*

*hear more accounts. Barbara was a vibrant young woman even before she left to find her fortune in the southern states. When she returned, married, but without a husband, everyone in the small community of Cannelton accepted her and her story. Inexplicitly, they rejoiced in it. Barbara was soft on sore eyes in this coal mining community. A crack shot, she reportedly took on and won in every marksmanship contest ever dared. A fine dancer, she was waited on in line at local community barn socials for dances in the spring and fall. These details are all we've been able to document by written account. Except for her oaken tombstone, also apparently referenced in papers:*

Loved by all,
Save One

*So read her wooden marker, according to newspaper accounts…long ago rotted away at her grave in the family cemetery plot, which is now also overgrown and neglected. It is still there, accessible through thick woods and with the right guide. Marked by crude stone, the family graves are a marvel to many who search. But Barbara's grave stands alone, off to the side, now without a marker, and sunken into the ground.*

*Here starts a story. Here begins the apparent decades of sightings… of helping, or of asking for help, from beyond. A tortured, yet poignant tale of unrequited warnings of evil in a hotbed. Here starts Barbara Davidson's story.*

*Barbara was not home when her family returned from Pittsburgh to buy livestock and feed in the autumn of 1795. She had been left alone to care for the homestead near the top of the Cannelton Valley but was nowhere to be found after their week-long journey. Her absence caused consternation and a search—the small but growing coal-mining community rallied to locate her. After ten days, her body was found by its rancid smell. It was under the floorboards of the family home front porch. Its head was missing.*

*Newspaper accounts corroborate this part of the story. The fact that Barbara's head and her murderer remain missing is true. Her estranged husband had an alibi states and miles away. In the village, no finger was ever pointed. It is one of America's oldest cold cases. And it never went away.*

*In the years since this cold-hearted murder, Barbara's ghost has appeared multiple times, and her story is the subject of newspaper articles. She sometimes materializes as a body with no head trying to relay a message. Occasionally she forms with a pig's head, supposedly taken from the family slaughterhouse to warn or scare people. And she lives on in this western Pennsylvania hamlet to this day.*

*During our first year of construction of the "Pig Lady Haunted Barn," the legend was a joke to us. I saw it as a nervous and laughed-off joke. Many a time, tools left for work the next day would disappear and reappear days later elsewhere. Before we'd wired in for electricity, we would call it quits at dusk and sometimes watch the fog roll in from the creek 200 yards away. Sometimes we would see shapes. And lights. And we would laugh them off, get into our trucks and drive away.*

*We kept on. Our Lions Club worked from mid-July until early October readying our new fundraiser. The first year was a success. Nearly $10,000 in gate revenues went to the Lions Club and from there to the less fortunate. Still, there were moments:*

Babe in the Woods, Haunted Barn promotion 2010. *Author's collection of Haunted Barn promotions.*

*Different colored lights on Indian Rock (a whole separate story). Objects levitated and thrown in the barn. Unexplained noises. Freaked-out kid actors. And then, finally, the sighting of Barbara's headless ghost—and the hearing of her garbled whispering voice—by three witnesses and a dozen others, via walkie-talkie.*

*One of the three witnesses of that last year—Tyler—was still in the truck with me tonight driving home. He didn't say anything. I guess Tyler didn't want to delve back into his story—one that had caused him ridicule for a year. The second, next to me, remained the same unnerving quiet he'd been since nearly two weeks ago. He wasn't the same.*

*His name is David. The 16-year-old sitting next to me, strangely mum, had had his own experience this year, and it was one we didn't want to hear again. It was over. For at least a year. We turned up the radio, talked about other stuff, and I delivered them to their homes. It was a long drive back to my house.*

This next account comes from a longtime western Pennsylvania resident now in his sixties. Occurring a full two generations before the Haunted Barn incident, this event is still fresh in the mind of the affected individual, now a member of the Little Beaver Historical Society.

I Went in Her Cave. *My experience with the Pig Lady occurred when I was about 12 or 13 years old. I first heard the story of the Pig Lady from my Uncle Norman. He was well-known as a practical joker and "tall tale teller" in our small hometown of Cannelton, Pa. Naturally, (being the cool and very mature 12-year-old I thought I was) I paid little attention to Uncle Norm's wild stories because he always enjoyed teasing me, so I was sure this was just a bunch of hooey.*

*Cannelton is a location where a somewhat rare type of coal, called Cannel Coal, was mined and therefore old coal mine shafts or "caves" were numerous throughout the area. One such cave opening was right along the side of the old dirt and gravel road that led up over what we called Cannelton Hill. At some point in time, my brother and I (and I believe my cousin) decided we would explore inside this old cave and see what was in* there. We found several old wooden crates, lots of old glass bottles and some old tin cans. We figured that a hobo had temporarily taken up residence there, but had long since moved on by the looks of things.

When we told good-ole Uncle Norm about our discovery, he said we were crazy for going in there and made us all promise to never go near there again because that's where the "Pig Lady" lives. That was enough to convince me to promise that I would never go near that cave again. (No problem!)

At the top of Cannelton Hill, there was a large house on the right that was once an old-school house where my mother and her brother (Uncle Norm) went to school as kids. This home was (at this time) occupied by a friend of mine and his family.

Sometime much later, I was up on top of Cannelton Hill visiting this friend, and while he and I played indoors that evening, I failed to realize it was getting somewhat dark. We had a strict rule in our home about being in our yard when it got dark. Upon seeing the darkness start to settle in, I began walking down the hill at a quick pace. Cannelton Hill had a very sharp curve about a fourth of the way down that we all called Hickory Nut Turn because of the large Hickory Nut Tree growing right there on the right-hand side of the old dirt and gravel road. Everything was going along just fine when suddenly something caught my eye in the direction of the old cave entrance about 20 yards from the side of the road just past Hickory Nut Turn. I immediately had thoughts of Uncle Norm telling us to never go near the cave again (especially after dark) since "that's where the Pig Lady lives."

Well, I was scared about half out of my mind now and was imagining all sorts of unsavory things. I thought I could hear the faint sounds of chains jingling and glass bottles clinking together, so I tried to place my feet down softly so I could tell if any footsteps were coming toward me or not. As I crept by as quietly as I could, I could not bring myself to turn my head and look directly at the cave entrance for fear of what I might see there. I thought to myself if that is the Pig Lady and she knows it was me that violated her cave, she might be angry with me and seeking to get even with me. I kept my head sort of down toward the road, and my eyes cut slightly to the right in case anyone (or anything) might be approaching from the direction of that darn cave.

Once I was about 20 yards past that cave, I quickly broke out into a full run as fast as I could go and never slowed down 'til I reached our front porch. As usual, Mom was sitting on her porch swing and said: "What *in the world is wrong with you? You act like you've just seen a ghost."* I said: *"Maybe I did."* *After she stopped laughing, she kept asking me what was wrong, so I told her I thought I might have seen the Pig Lady up on Cannelton Hill. She said it was apparent I had been listening to my Uncle Norm's silly made-up stories, and there was nothing to it at all.*

*Mom did her best to convince me that the whole Pig Lady story was just another wild story concocted by her brother to frighten us kids and keep us from going into those old coal mines. Until only recently, I had spent nearly my whole life believing that the Pig Lady was nothing but pure fabrication and there was never a shred of truth to it. Now it seems there may be at least "some" truth in this story. Who would have ever imagined after all this time, that someone would/could dig up evidence that this story is based on a true-life incident way back before the Civil War? Who knew? Clearly, not me.*

Barbara's ghost isn't always the tormentor in Cannelltonite stories. Another more malevolent entity is sometimes witnessed, lending some to believe Barbara's killer still roams Cannelton's fields and hillsides, causing Barbara's

Red Hill Mine, 2017.

restless soul to remain to warn the living. The following is the childhood narrative of a Darlington, Pennsylvania resident, also in his sixties, who grew up in Cannelton. The author, an avowed skeptic and a past El Camino enthusiast, to this day has no explanation for what occurred.

> Red Eyes. *I swore I'd never tell anyone about the Pig Lady. And, except for a few close friends, I haven't. Honestly, I'm not sure I've ever even told my wife. Probably shouldn't now.*
>
> *Over the years, I've sometimes recalled the encounter and have always immediately tried to justify it in some reasonable, rational way. I'm not crazy. But it did happen. And it wasn't any hallucination or hysteria or from 14-year-old hormones or drugs or alcohol or lighting or over-active imagination or trickery or anything else. It happened.*
>
> *It was late August. Summer was ending, a new school year was about to restart, and I was tired of the older guys making fun of me for not being able to dive off the Hippie Bridge. The water there was not all that deep, and a 9-foot dive into it was—daunting. But my friend Steve and I had suffered the taunts of the older guys for too long. I had to learn. Alone.*
>
> *You couldn't drive or even ride your bike back there then. So, I left my 10-speed by the cable that roped off the access, maybe a half-mile from the bridge. After 10 minutes standing on the edge of the worn boards (forever), I made one dive. It was terrible. I'd tried to remember everything the guys had said about using my legs for the launch and my hands to make it shallow, but it didn't work. I sprained my wrists on the bottom just before my head hit the sandy rocks and nearly knocked me out. I was lucky to have survived it.*
>
> *I gathered my gear and started the trek back to my bike in the grassy lane. It was a calm dusk. I remember thinking how quiet it was. Almost immediately, I had the sense someone was watching. I shook it off. But then I heard something walking parallel to me. Close. Maybe 40 or 50 feet in the woods. I stopped. It stopped. I started. It started. I was walking on grass; it was making its way through the underbrush. I was creeping. It wasn't. It couldn't, there in that terrain. I started again, watching this time. I heard it, and I saw it.*
>
> *It was much closer than I'd guessed. Maybe 20 or 25 feet in, just beyond the briars and weeds that clogged the side of the road. I only saw its eye—a red eye—and then only occasionally as it dipped under branches and squinted against fall leaves and twigs. It was its right eye. I was on the right, on the road, and it was on my left.*

Restored Hippie Bridge, 2018.

Red Eyes: approximate location for the encounter.

*I stopped. It stopped. Then I couldn't see it. I began to question my senses and mindset. I thought I was hallucinating—and that that was interesting because I'd never experienced this before.*

*Then this: I thought of the legend of the Pig Lady. I'd grown up with it, having grown up in Cannelton. I knew, for example, that all the older guys used the story to scare their dates into snuggling. I knew what my Dad and other adults had told me. I knew, somehow, it was her.*

*This is stupid, I thought, and wiped my face with my towel and started running. It started running. I ran faster; it ran faster. I was on a clear path, illuminated by the day's last light. It was crashing through dead branches, stomping on twigs and leaves and not caring about stealth. I was scared. I ran faster yet; it faltered but kept up. It tripped and almost fell once and sort of squealed—just a short note—but I remember it. It paralleled me no matter how fast I went. I jogged, it jogged. I slowed; it slowed. I stopped. I yelled—I was scared out of my mind, alone and helpless against who knows what this was. I screamed—as loud as my fear would allow—three things:*

*"WHAT ARE YOU?"*

*"WHO ARE YOU??"*

*"WHAT DO YOU WANT???"*

*Then I saw both its eyes. It had turned to face me. They were as red as a spotlighted animal, though I wasn't using a light. They were as high as mine, level, close to six feet in height. They were calm.*

*And then they changed. As I watched, transfixed, the eyes squinted, bending and slitting upward—not in a mean way, but happy, as though they were smiling. We stared unblinkingly for what seemed like forever.*

*It was right there. I could've hit it with a rock. I could've jumped the drainage ditch and met it head-on. It was as real as this keyboard, and I knew it then, and I know it now. It had followed me, and now it was right there looking at me and smiling. I don't know why. I only know it happened.*

*I ran the 500 yards to my bike, cleared the fence, turned my bike, mounted it and pedaled home as fast as I could, maybe faster. I didn't sleep that night; my Mom could tell the next morning. She asked what was up, what was going on. I said nothing.*

Another anecdote follows, transcribed by Rich Oswald, recounting a confrontation with the probable spectral form of Barbara's killer. It is unknown why this malicious entity apparently remains in the hills and fields near Barbara's alleged grave.

*It's Just a Dream. Isn't it?* Icy hands clenched like a vise on her throat. The girl choked. Gasped desperately to breathe. She tried to reach out, but her arms were unable to respond. As she looked to her tormentor, his yellow demonic eyes relished her helplessness. The dark lips of his cruel scimitar mouth parted slightly, the putrid smell of rotten flesh. Somehow, she managed a strangled scream, and she was once again awake and alone in her bedroom.

This scene had repeated itself over and over almost every night since Carol had moved into the trailer in Cannelton with her younger fourteen-year-old sister Colleen—the same home her parents had purchased and rented out to numerous tenants over the past five years. It was their attempt at a bit of independence from Mom and Dad. It seemed the right thing at the time, but now Carol was not so sure. These recurring nightmares were so real. There were times she woke up with red finger marks on her throat. She convinced herself that somehow, she must have done it to herself in her sleep. Eventually, the marks would disappear.

Then there were the visions; they seemed so real.

There were times Carol would wake up in her bed with the distinct feeling there was someone in the room with her. She could smell the musky perspiration that pervaded the place; the dank odor of a man who had not bathed for days. Carol wanted to close her eyes and will away the image that she knew was to come, but she knew she had to look. Ignoring the presence of the awful man in the room would not change a thing.

The girl would then force open her eyes, hoping just this one time he would not be there. But each time, there in the corner of the room, stood a dark hulking figure, wearing an oversized, misshapen floppy-brimmed hat. Sometimes she saw the evil flash of his eyes, but mostly he was the same dark shadow that took up the corner nearly to the ceiling. The man, for a long time, would just stand there motionless. Carol knew from her past experiences it was useless to flee. She had tried on many occasions, but her legs, as well as her arms, would not move. Then the figure would slowly advance toward her, and she could see his features more distinctly. His face, it seemed the same size and shape of a ham, and it was shiny with sweat. His matted beard and long stringy black hair tied back by oily leather thongs slicked with some foul-smelling, greasy crud. It was then that Carol's insides turned to jelly.

From beneath his heavily soiled cloak, he drew a knife—with the most wicked-looking blade, she could imagine. With a crooked smile and a tilt of the head, the man would make a harsh whistling sound between his teeth like a steaming tea kettle. Then he would be looking eye to eye with his victim.

*Heh heh heh I got you now!* It would rasp malevolently.

Carol had many times convinced herself this was all a dream—a rather realistic and scary one for sure. Staying at the trailer together this summer with Colleen had been a bold move on her part—living without their parents for the first time. Surely the anxiety of this transition was playing havoc with her imagination. Of course, she convinced herself that was it. But Carol knew she was just lying to herself. Sometimes she wondered if she was going insane. That would have been the perfect explanation. But Carol didn't think there was anything wrong with her mentally. Everything was normal in her life—until dark that is.

She had convinced herself that maybe the best thing would be to tell Colleen what was going on and get out of this place, but her ego stood in the way. How could she admit to her little sister that she could not cut it away from Mom and Dad? And besides, this was just a dream. Right?

After several weeks of the same thing—night after night, Carol's nerves frayed to the breaking point. Then she, just by chance had the opportunity to talk with Frank, the custodian at the trailer court one evening around twilight.

"Not a good idea to be by yourself here, now is it, young lady? People see strange things around here what with the cemetery and all."

"Cemetery? What cemetery is that, Frank?" asked Carol.

"The one right across from here. Over there…" Frank pointed to a low hill with a grove of trees across the road from the trailer court. "They say it's haunted. Lots of people say it."

"You're kidding of course," whispered Carol.

"Not at all. You've heard of Barbara Davidson, I presume."

"No, I haven't."

"Well, that's where she's buried. No head, they say."

"Pardon? No head?"

"Right. Had it cut off. Some say Barbara floats around here some nights looking for it."

"Say," Carol pursued a bit nonchalantly, "there aren't others around—like a huge man with a knife?"

Frank turned to her, a bit pale it seemed. "You've seen this man?"

Carol laughed nervously. "Only in my dreams, I think."

Frank shuffled his feet and looked across at the old cemetery. "Did you ever wonder why your folks can't keep tenants in their place? Every one of them has had some bad experiences, but none last more than a month or so. If I were you, I'd get out and have your folks get rid of the place."

A cold chill ran up Carol's spine. Could this dream be real?

Suddenly a curdling scream came from the direction of the trailer—a cry that she knew could only have come from her younger sister who had been asleep in her room.

"Oh no, God, no, not Colleen!"

Carol was across the vacant lot between her and the trailer so fast she didn't remember her feet touching the ground. For what felt like an eternity she pulled frantically on the front door that seemed frozen shut. Finally, she and Frank opened the door to a pale-faced Colleen.

"Oh Carol, it's so awful! It's a terrible man in my room, and he wants to kill me. I just know it! He has a knife, and he says he has me now! It's not a dream—I know it's real! I don't want ever to go in there again. I'm so scared!"

Both girls were shaking, locked in a firm embrace. Frank had a large silver flashlight, and its beam was flashing back through the darkened bedroom.

"Nothing—nothing in there girls…"

When Frank turned both Carol and Colleen were getting in Carol's VW. The engine whined to life, and the two girls disappeared, wide-eyed toward home.

That trailer was never rented again. The two sisters often related their experiences afterward and had wondered many times about the other spirits that were said to be haunting the old cemetery near the trailer court.

# THE PLAYERS

This research quickly becomes difficult to follow because of the substantial number of people involved and their potential interconnections. To continue this peek behind the analytic process curtain, it's necessary to provide a cast of characters for the reader to reference if needed. I'm only supplying this as part of the Pig Lady deep dive. The stories in the following chapters are more polished executive-style finished products and do not include this feature.

## *The McCaskeys*

*Barbara*
- Married name Davidson
- Barbara is the story's alleged murder victim

*Samuel*
- Barbara's immediate relative, either her father or brother

*Mary*
- Either Barbara's sister or sister-in-law

*William*
- A probable relative of Samuel and Barbara

## *The Davidsons*

*Nathan*
- Barbara's supposed husband

*Joseph*
- Possibly Nathan's brother
- A close acquaintance of William McCaskey and John Hughes

*Nancy*
- John Hughes's wife and daughter of old Mrs. Davidson

*Mary*
- Possible sister of Joseph and Nathan
- Possibly Barbara McCaskey's sister-in-law

*Old Mrs. Davidson*
- John Hughes's mother-in-law
- Nancy Davidson's mother
- A close acquaintance of William McCaskey

*William Davidson*
- Revolutionary War officer
- Father of children named Nathan, Joseph, Nancy and Mary Davidson

## The Neighbors

*George Foulks*
- Northwest Indian War veteran
- Brother of William Foulks
- Uncle of Charlie Foulks

*William Foulks*
- Revolutionary War militiaman
- The first Beaver County settler north of the Ohio River and west of the Beaver River
- Captain in the Ohio Militia in the War of 1812

*Ben Franklin and Jack McMasters*
- Samuel McCaskey's counterfeiting partners

*John Hughes*
- Barbara Davidson's landlord and husband of Nancy Davidson

# Robin Hood's Wraith

The earliest accounts of encounters with Barbara's ghost, according to Oswald, are available from 1800 on, but this researcher could not locate any of those initial versions. I did, however, acquire an original copy from 1914 provided by arguably Cannelton's most celebrated son, Ira Mansfield:

> *Near the opening of Cannel coal mine, three ravines meet with small rivulets and rocky falls, marking a dark but lovely spot. The music of Whip-poor-will falls, coupled with the groans of "Oohche, Eacchi," from beech fiddle trees as the wind sways them together makes the cry of dying victims. Here the first McCaskeys settled in 1793. The father, a Whig, was killed in South Carolina and the family driven into exile by the Tories and British dragoons under Tarleton. The family located a settler's claim over the Cannel mine, building a log cabin also clearing few acres of land. One of the daughters named Barbara was handsome and had two suitors. One morning Barbara was found murdered and her head missing. Her ghost is erratic, sometimes the body, or only the head appearing at unlooked for times and places. Only a few years ago, a driver of a four-horse team related in all sincerity an encounter with Barbara. Coming down the crossroads from Hell's Hollow Tavern, he observed a*

*dark figure and when right opposite the apparition, it sprang upon the back of the off-wheel horse—a gray beast that enabled him to observe the outlines of a headless woman. On reaching the old McCaskey cabin site, the woman sprang off and disappeared in a glow of bright light. What convinced the driver that there was no deception, although a cold night his horses were in a lather of sweat and trembling and ever afterward his team would shy on passing this cabin.*[18]

Mansfield passed away in 1919, but his name is still well known in the area. A close look at both Mansfield's and Oswald's versions of the story reveals some modifications, but that is not surprising. Folklore often morphs with time like a children's game of telephone. For example, a close look at the New International Version versus the King James Bible reveals variations:

*Luke 2:33*
*And Joseph and his mother marveled at those things which were spoken of him.*

*Luke 2:33*
*The child's father and mother marveled at what was said about him.*

One can assume Jesus's father is Joseph in the latter, but it is implied he is not in the former. The point here is not to debate which is correct, but to show that stories, even the most revered, change over time. Because of this, slight alterations to Barbara's tale are foreseeable. Of particular note, Mansfield's account of Barbara's alleged murder does not discuss the probable reason her story lives on in oral tradition. For that, we turn to Thomas White's interview of Rich Oswald.

*Stories are told of young people seeing a strange woman in the distance, but when they approach, she turns and reveals the grinning face of a pig. Sometimes the apparition is accompanied by a grunting sound, such as a pig might make. The Pig Lady has been spotted all around the Cannelton area, including the north-fork of the Little Beaver River, referred to locally as the "Hippie Bridge." While recording stories of these alleged encounters, Oswald discovered two theories as to why Barbara's ghost would appear with the head of a pig. One postulates that since Barbara raised livestock and took care of pigs on her parents' farm, she selected the "replacement head" of an animal she had worked closely with. A second theory speculates that her ghost wandered for a long time in search of a head. Eventually, she encountered either the severed head of a slaughtered pig or the head of a dead wild pig and chose it to replace her own. The story of the pig head has become so popular that Barbara's ghost is often referred to only as the Pig Lady.*[19]

Would Barbara's story still be as popular today without this fantastic detail? How many Beaver or Columbiana County residents can honestly say they are aware of the equally grisly and well-documented life of local pioneer George Foulks, who at eleven years old was kidnapped by Wyandot Indians after they brutally tomahawked and scalped several neighbors and family members?[20] George later escaped to freedom and became a military scout under General "Mad" Anthony Wayne in the Northwest Indian War, but now a fair number of Beaver County residents only know his former farm property as the alleged burial place of the Pig Lady.

## Analysis of Evidence: The Timeline

The first step toward forming a viable hypothesis when performing analysis is determining the credibility of available sources. Judgments based on misunderstood information cannot be presented as reliable. Regardless of the purported paranormal affairs encircling Barbara Davidson's story, if a crime did occur, then some evidence could remain. With this in mind, an examination of the timeline reveals inconsistencies.

In Oswald's version of the story, Barbara and her family settled in Pennsylvania after the Revolutionary War sometime before 1791. Mansfield's telling of the story has the McCaskeys arriving in 1793. To ascertain which is more likely to be correct, we need to better understand the state of affairs in the territory at the time.

American settlers were not legally permitted to settle on Indian lands in the Northwest Territory (to include the northern part of Beaver County) until the Treaty of Fort Macintosh in 1785. This line of demarcation was enforced by the military, as noted in the following letter from General Brodhead—commander of the Western Department during the Revolution—to General George Washington.[21]

*Pittsburgh, Oct. 26, 1779.*

*Dear Gen'l:*
*Immediately after I had closed my last (of the 9th of this instant), I rec'd a letter from Col. Shepard Lieut. Of Ohio County, informing me that a certain Decker, Cox & Company with others had crossed the Ohio River, and committed trespasses on the Indians' lands wherefore I ordered sixty Rank and File to be equipped & Capt. Clarke of the 8th Pen' Reg't proceeded with this party to Wheeling, with orders to cross the River at that part, & to apprehend some of the principle trespassers, and destroy the Hutts. He returned without finding any of the trespassers but destroyed some Hutts. He writes me that inhabitants have made small improvements all the way from the Muskingum River to Fort McIntosh & thirty miles up some of the Branches. I sent a runner to the Delaware Council at Coochocking* [Coshocton, Ohio] *to inform them of the trespass & assure them it was committed by some foolish people & requested them to rely on my doing them justice & punishing the offenders, but as yet have not received an answer.*

Later, General Irvine delivered an even more stern warning from Fort Pitt.

*Order, Fort Pitt, February 25, 1783.*
*Any person who shall presume to ferry either men or women over the Ohio or Allegheny rivers or shall be found crossing over into what is generally called the Indian country between the Kittanning and Fort MacIntosh without written permission from the commanding officer at Fort Pitt, orders for that purpose—until further orders shall be treated and prosecuted for holding or aiding others to correspond with and give intelligence to, the enemy. This order to be enforced until civil government thinks proper to direct otherwise.*

The Northwest Indian wars raged from 1785 through 1795, with arguably the deadliest years on the Pennsylvania frontier occurring from 1789 to 1792. During that time, land north of the Ohio River was contested between the newly formed United States of America and several Native American nations not included in previous treaty negotiations. Britain had ceded the Northwest Territory to the United States in 1783 but refused to vacate a few militarily strategic locations, such as Fort Detroit. Motivated by a desire to create an Indian buffer state in the region between the United States and

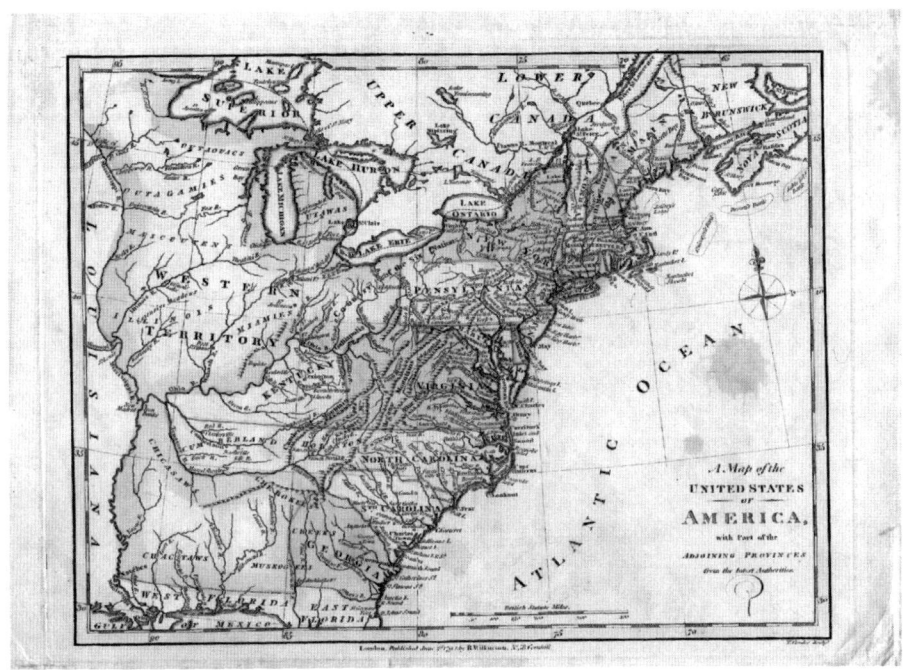

Map of the United States, 1791.

British Canada, British troops trained and supplied Native American tribes in what essentially became a proxy war. Countless atrocities were committed on both sides.

America was not yet strong enough to exert dominion over the area. The United States hadn't expanded much beyond the original thirteen colonial regions, but some states had surveyed and begun selling tracts of the disputed territory. Pennsylvania, in particular, set aside a large section of the lands, called the Depreciation Tract, still claimed by northwestern tribes in 1785.[22] The state planned to use these lands, which included what would become Cannelton, to compensate its Revolutionary War veterans for their service; however, clashes with natives made settlement difficult. On March 25, 1791, General Presley Neville wrote to Governor Mifflin:

> *On the 18th one man killed and 13 prisoners taken above Pittsburgh, and on the 23rd thirteen men, women and children (mostly the latter) were killed 15 miles above the river on the same river (I believe at the mouth of Bull Creek) which has so alarmed the Frontiers, that I fear they will break up. The settlement on the Depreciation tract amounting to about forty to fifty*

*families has fled to a Man, and many on the Ohio have moved to more interior situations. The militia is in great want of arms. I do not believe that more than one-sixth are provided for. Five or six years of continued peace had destroyed all thoughts of defense, and the game became scarce, and arms have slipped off to Kentucky and other later settlements, where there appeared to be more use for them.*

*The Corn Planter and his party (about forty-five in number) are now ascending the Alleghany River to their Country. They left Pittsburgh four days ago. The first murder on the Allegheny was committed in one mile of his camp, and he was not distant from the other. Notwithstanding his professions* [Chief Corn Planter was considered an ally at the time], *some of his party are greatly suspected, at least of being confederate in this business, and parties have been forming to pursue and cut them off. However, I hope it may not be carried into effect, it would add the Seneca's to our enemies; already too numerous for our defenseless frontiers, and the settlement on the French Creek would be an immediate sacrifice.* \*

The conflict subsided enough by early 1792 that civilians could settle in relative safety in what later became Beaver County. The first permanent settler in the county north of the Ohio River was George Foulks's older brother William. Settling in South Beaver Township in April 1792, William served in the Pennsylvania militia and may have earned his land claim through service, but I could not locate proof of this. Considering he probably never served in the Continental army, it's more likely that William claimed his land as a settler under the Vacant Land Act. Passed into state law on April 3, 1792, the act provided two pathways for acquiring vacant territory in western Pennsylvania, either by traveling to available land tracts directly and making settlements and improvements to the land or by purchasing warrants at the land office in Philadelphia and having the land in the warrants officially surveyed. William is also associated with Beaver County's first murder trial. In November 1807, William's neighbor or farmhand, according to conflicting reports, killed a member of a posse sent to remove William from his property due to a land ownership dispute. He was later acquitted.[23]

---

\* An ally of the British, Seneca chief Corn Planter fought in both the French and Indian and American Revolutionary Wars. Afterward, Corn Planter led peace negotiations with the United States and was integral in maintaining Iroquois neutrality during the Northwest Indian War.

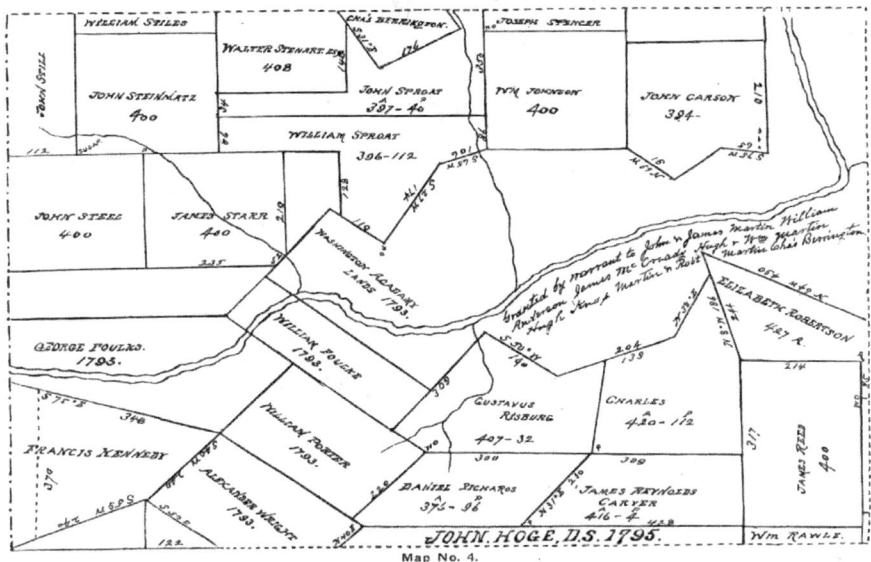

Cannelton Area Survey (now Darlington and South Beaver Townships) map, 1795; Foulks's properties are in the left middle. *Little Beaver Historical Society.*

George Foulks earned a Depreciation tract* for his service as an Indian scout under the fearsome Captain Samuel Brady during the Northwest Indian War.[24] George's tract, straddling both sides of the creek, was surveyed for him in 1793 while George was still serving in the military, but he didn't inhabit his land until the spring of 1797.[†25] That year, he built a log cabin and one of the first water-powered mills in the region. The foundation of this mill, along with the footing for a stone house he built later, are still visible today. In 1820, "He built the first brick house in that section of the country," according to Bausman's *History of Beaver County*.[26] This home, later known as the Fennell house, became the setting for a less familiar legend described in chapter 5 of this book. Rich Oswald's version of the Pig Lady story suggests she is buried in the Foulks family burial ground on this property.

---

* Veterans who had served in the Continental forces in the Pennsylvania Line or Pennsylvania navy or who had been prisoners of war were eligible to receive what were known as "depreciation certificates." Lands in the area immediately north of Pittsburgh, located between the Ohio and Allegheny Rivers, were sold to raise money to underwrite these depreciation certificates. Although the Northwest Indian Wars were considered a continuation of the Revolution, George's later claim for a military pension was denied, as he didn't actively fight the British.
† George Foulks likely served in the military until sometime after the Treaty of Greenville, ending the war in August 1795.

Foulks'/Watt's Mill foundation, 2017.

Considering the historical record, it is unlikely that any Americans legally resided on lands that would eventually become Cannelton prior to 1792, as suggested by Mr. Oswald's version of the story. However, this doesn't necessarily mean squatters weren't living in Cannelton before 1793, when Depreciation Tract land surveys began there. Both versions of Barbara's story reference Samuel, but recall that in Mansfield's, Barbara's father died in South Carolina. Oswald's narrative asserts Samuel was Barbara's father, but Mansfield never clarifies the relationship between Barbara and Samuel. Mansfield also claims several times in other essays that Samuel McCaskey and his early neighbors were criminals. In describing his Cannel Coal Farm, Mansfield wrote:

> *Take the P. L. & W. cars, within an hour from either terminal, and you are there. Passing Union Church, stores, opera house, unpaved streets, we come to the homestead. Bancroft's History relates that in 1753, here runners from Gen Washington found Chief Tanacharisson hunting wild turkeys. In the old home are collections of Indian and war relics. Nearby is the Wedding Cave, that disclosed stolen garments and jewelry, also the 1754 cannel opening where Barbara's ghost resides. Passing the two whip-poor-will falls, along rows of majestic white pines, we come to Bald Knob*

*at an altitude of 1250, giving views across Pennsylvania into Ohio and Virginia.\* Alongside are Indian burying grounds; orchards over one mile in length, and remains of McCaskey, Ben Franklin and McMasters' cabins, who were expert thieves and counterfeiters. The only way to them was by the "Hell's hollow road."*[27]

Mansfield noted further McCaskey-associated criminal activity and the Foulks burial ground in a separate essay about chicken theft:

*Samuel Caskey [sic] and Ben Franklin, who resided in Cannelton orchards, introduced the first Leghorns, having stolen a crate of twenty-six in Pittsburgh. They were arrested, plead guilty and fined sixty dollars. They paid the fine in silver dollars, of their own make, that had no silver in them, escaping further trouble. When Ben Franklin died, we discovered his molds, ladles and some money in a secret cave under his Leghorn chicken houses, and they were buried with him, in the old Foulk's graveyard across the Little Beaver Creek from Watt's Mills.*†[28]

The age of Barbara's mother is another significant timeline disparity between Mansfield's and Oswald's versions of the story. Mansfield suggests Mrs. McCaskey was still winning athletic competitions in 1820; if the timeline as laid out by Oswald is correct, she would have given birth to Barbara forty-three years prior. Then again, Mansfield also claims she was a witch.

*Tradition relates that the mother of the ghostly Mary and Barbara McCaskey outran and outjumped every soldier in the Annual Military Encampment of 1820.*[29]

*Dame Caskey, the redoubtable witch at Candle Coal*‡ *orchards, was always in demand and present when sickness and death invaded the early families along the Little Beaver. Many believed her specially prepared candles, when lighted and placed around the corpse, would ward off evil spirits.*[30]

---

\* Mansfield often refers to West Virginia as Virginia. The state formed from Virginia's western counties that sided with the North during the Civil War in 1863.
† Rueben Watt became proprietor of George Foulks's grist and sawmills in 1863, more than two decades after George's death in 1840. Prior to that, George's daughter Charlotte and son-in-law George Huffman owned the land.
‡ Candle coal is a nickname for cannel coal.

Mr. Oswald's story claims Barbara's murder took place in 1795, and the abandoned cannel coal mines may be the location of her discarded head.[31] However, the first commercial mine in Cannelton didn't open until 1838.[32] Oswald's account of the story also asserts Barbara married a military veteran from Virginia, Nathan Davidson, in 1791. While some might find it odd that a Virginian would be on the Pennsylvania frontier in 1791, West Virginia was still part of Virginia until 1863, meaning he wouldn't have had to travel far to meet Barbara. The West Virginia border is less than twenty-five miles from Cannelton. Moreover, Virginia and Pennsylvania held competing claims for much of the territory south of Pittsburgh until 1785. Yohogania County, Virginia, included much of today's Beaver County, Pennsylvania, south of the Ohio River, until the dispute became resolved in 1785. The strong governing authorities of the British colonies and then state affairs early on, as opposed to a central national government, molded regional identities in America's populations early on. Therefore, many living in the region before 1785 still claimed to be Virginians long afterward.

Additionally, Virginian and Pennsylvanian militia and regular military units operated from forts and blockhouses all along the Ohio River, protecting the frontier during the Revolutionary and Northwest Indian Wars. One can assume this is how William and George knew about the most fertile lands to claim in and around Cannelton. Fort Macintosh, in what is now Beaver, Pennsylvania, closed in 1791. The United States' first basic military training grounds at Legionville near present-day Baden, Pennsylvania, was established the following year to equip and train General Anthony Wayne's Legion of the United States. This army would eventually defeat the Western Confederacy of Indians at the Battle of Fallen Timbers in 1794, ending the Northwest Indian War.[33]

The principal timeline disparity between the two versions of the story appears in another Mansfield essay, this one detailing a quitclaim deed filed in 1833 by John Hughes that names both Samuel McCaskey and Barbara Davidson living on the property after May 1799.*

> *The tract described in this deed is located on the Little Beaver Creek two miles east of the Ohio line in Darlington Township. John Hughes filed settlement with Justices Martin and Cochran, placing as tenants John Bridgeman in May 1799, followed by Alexander Jacob Smith, Henry Crowl and Barbara Davidson, who was later found in her cabin with her head missing, and her ghost still haunts this locality. The five settlement*

---

* A quitclaim deed is a legal procedure for the transfer of property.

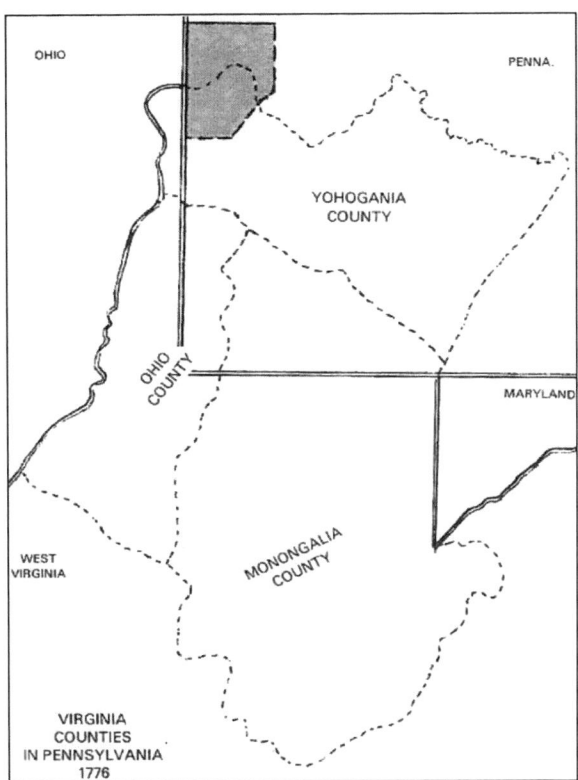

*Right*: Virginia counties in Pennsylvania. Shaded section is modern Beaver County. *From* The Beaver County Bicentennial Atlas. *Beaver, PA: Beaver County Bicentennial Commission.*

*Below*: Fort McIntosh.

*cabins on Cannel coal tract, a rendezvous for horse thieves and counterfeiters. Samuel McCaskey, Jack McMasters, and Ben Franklin, each serving a term in the state penitentiary for making "lead money" at Cannel mines.*[34]

While not stated outright, it appears that Mansfield is claiming the first settler on the property was John Bridgeman in 1799 and that Barbara married and was murdered sometime after then. I failed to locate documentation of this purported crime. The absence of records is notable, however—if no arrests or trial occurred, as suggested by Mr. Oswald, then records might never have been available. Law enforcement in the region was sporadic early on, so arrest proceedings and court records of crimes are difficult to find. The county's first sheriff, William Henry, wasn't elected until 1804, and he operated from the county seat at Beaver, which was a fifteen-mile journey by horse.[35] Beaver County's first newspaper didn't begin to cover local events until late 1807, right around the same time as Beaver County's first murder trial in November of that year.[36]

In researching the story, I managed to locate an additional piece of questionable timeline-based evidence that weakens confidence in Ira's narrative. Mr. Mansfield used a photograph of a tombstone to illustrate a story about Barbara's alleged ghostly sister in one of his books.

*Barbara's sister, Mary, afterward married and is buried just across the Ohio state line. Even after death, Mary continued a "Xantippe of a wife" and troubled her husband by ghostly appearances.\* To appease her spirit, the tormented husband erected the elaborate headstone, a picture of which appears at the head of this article.*[37]

The grave in the photo is still standing in Poland, Ohio, Ira Mansfield's place of birth, and curiously it's located in the same cemetery in which Mansfield's brother and other relatives are buried—calling into question the credibility of this piece of evidence.† Mansfield was interested in graveyards, writing essays about epitaphs and local cemeteries in his two most admired books.[38] Mansfield's photograph of Mary's marker cuts off the lower half of the stone. The full inscription reveals that this Mary died in 1846 at the age of twenty-seven, meaning she was born in 1818. If this were Barbara's sister, she'd be significantly younger than Barbara. While Poland is just across the

---

\* Xantippe was Socrates's wife, remembered for being exceptionally nagging and shrewish.
† A monument to Poland, Ohio's forty-niners erected by Ira that includes his grandfather's name is also located here.

*Left*: Barbara's sister. *Photo by Ira Mansfield; from Mansfield,* Historical Collections: Little Beaver River Valleys.

*Right*: Mary Ragan.

Mansfield and Morse graves with Mary in the background.

state line, as mentioned by Mansfield, it's a suspicious coincidence that this stone is in a graveyard that contains many of his relatives. Although it is feasible that Barbara's sister married an Ohio man named Ragan and is interred among Mansfield's family members, it's more likely that he noticed Mary Ragan's gravestone on one of his visits and chose to use it to enrich the story.

## Analysis of Evidence: Source Derivation

Every great storyteller is a master of embellishment, especially when evidentiary information isn't readily available. Conversely, it is significant that Mansfield's version of Barbara's story is probably the first preserved in print, and like most folklore, it may be loosely based on tangible events. Ira Mansfield learned of Barbara's story and other accounts of Cannelton's first settlers from primary sources, one of which was Robin Hood Club member Charley Foulks, son of William Foulks and nephew of George.[39] Because the McCaskeys and Davidsons lived near George, Charley most likely learned the story of Barbara's murder directly from one of the original Cannelton settlers. Because of this, one can reasonably argue that oral history descending directly from Foulks provenance carries weight.

Unlike Mr. Oswald, Mansfield never claims Barbara is buried in the Foulks family graveyard, but he casually mentions that Barbara's former next-door neighbor (and Samuel McCaskey's partner in crime) Ben Franklin is buried there.[40] This connection suggests a second primary source for Mr. Mansfield's version of the story exists. By claiming, "When Ben Franklin died, we discovered his (counterfeiting) molds," Mansfield indicates that he knew Franklin personally, or at the very least he assisted his aunt and uncle in clearing out their former tenant's property after Franklin died. Mansfield began operating his widowed aunt Morse's Cannelton coal mine, orchard and tenant properties upon returning from the Civil War in 1865, buying it outright in 1870. Mansfield would have been six years old when his uncle Edwin Morse purchased the property in 1848. Depending on when Franklin passed on and assuming Ira Mansfield visited his aunt and uncle in his youth, it is probable that Mansfield and his relatives knew Barbara's former neighbor.

The now entirely forested Foulks family burial ground comprises at least half a dozen unmarked fieldstones among markers engraved with several different surnames, none of which are Foulks. Any headboards—wooden

Edwin Morse's grave in Poland, Ohio.

*Left*: Huffman infant grave marker. *Right*: George Foulks gravestone.

grave markers commonly used in the seventeenth and eighteenth centuries for low-income interments—would have decomposed long ago. The newest tomb on the property belongs to a Civil War veteran named Howells. The burial ground eventually became unkempt, which may be the reason George Foulks's body was exhumed and moved to the Glenview Cemetery in East Palestine, Ohio, near the graves of his father-in-law, daughter and son-in-law. Of the inscribed headstones that remain, the only Foulks family members I can identify are a grandson or granddaughter named Huffman who passed in 1851 during infancy and Henry Cline, an in-law of George's eldest daughter, Elizabeth.*

It's unusual for a family graveyard to contain disparate surnames. George apparently knew his neighbors intimately. His farm and mill may have furnished employment for early Canneltonites before the commercial coal mines opened.† It stands to reason that if Franklin is buried in this location, then Barbara is too, as suggested by Oswald.

---

* George's daughter Charlotte married George Huffman and inherited George's brick home after he passed in 1840. Henry Cline died in 1823.
† The first coal mine in Cannelton opened in 1838, just two years prior to George Foulks's death.

## Analysis of Evidence: Supplemental Sources

Typically, validation of conflicting or questionable source material can only occur by corroborating points of credible information, but in this case, factual data is scarce. Collection of census information for the county began in 1800 but listed only the heads of household (usually men) until 1850. Nevertheless, some circumstantial evidence is attainable. One particularly interesting piece comes from a May 4, 1827 diary entry written by Reverend Robert Dilworth, traveling pastor of the Little Beaver Church. Reverend Dilworth merely notes, "William McCaskey called and informed us that old Mrs. Davidson (John Hughes mother-in-law) died this evening."[41] It is uncertain how or if William McCaskey is a relative of Barbara Davidson or Samuel McCaskey, but the disclosure by a McCaskey that John Hughes—Barbara's landlord—was also married to a Davidson is hard to pass off as coincidence. Reverend Dilworth's diary notes many events in the Little Beaver Creek Valley from 1820 to 1868, including the date the reverend performed a marriage ceremony for one of George Foulks's daughters to another man named Davidson.* Later, an entry accurately describes George's time and cause of death in 1840, validating the diary's authenticity.

The Mansfield "Abstracts" essay noted earlier lists all land records related to his Cannelton coal mine properties from the first Depreciation Tract land survey in 1793 through his purchase of the lands in 1870. Barbara's lone mention is in the abstract cited earlier, but Samuel McCaskey is included again as a defendant in a later abstract describing an ejectment suit (eviction) filed against him and a few others in 1847 by trustees of the U.S. Bank after they acquired the property through James Patterson via John Hughes's heirs. John died in 1844.[42] In his will, he left one-third of his property to his wife, Nancy (Davidson) Hughes. Signatory witnesses to John's last will and testament include the same Reverend Robert Dilworth and William McCaskey, further reinforcing that the McCaskey and Davidson families were possibly related. Another sad series of Reverend Dilworth's diary entries seem to suggest corroborating evidence of this familial relationship.

> *2nd Jan 1836—Mr. May called early and said that Joseph Davidson's third child died suddenly. Attended the funeral. Heard that he had another child very ill with scarlet fever.*

---

* Rebecca Foulks married Jesse Davidson at George Foulks's home in Cannelton on December 23, 1830.

*3rd Jan 1836—Mr. May called and said that another child of Joseph Davidson's died before daylight, and 3 or 4 of Wm. McCaskey's children are ill with scarlet fever.*

*10th Jan 1836—Heard that Joseph Davidson had a third child die in the morning.*

If Joseph Davidson, Old Mrs. Davidson (John Hughes's mother-in-law) and John Hughes's wife, Nancy, were intimately acquainted with William McCaskey (potentially Samuel and Barbara McCaskey's relative), then something can be learned by researching this line of the Davidson family. Better genealogic information would prove useful, but thus far the data I've uncovered is circumstantial.

In Philadelphia, on May 29, 1827, Joseph, son of Captain William Davidson of the Third Pennsylvania Regiment, filed a claim for a three-hundred-acre tract in western Pennsylvania.[43] Captain Davidson was captured by the British and likely died a prisoner of war at Fort Washington. The claim made on behalf of Captain Davidson's immediate family also included his widowed wife, Lydia, son Nathan and four daughters, Lydia, Sarah, Nancy and Mary. My research failed to determine whether or not Nancy Davidson, wife of John Hughes, was the daughter of Captain Davidson, or if the Joseph Davidson mentioned in Reverend Dilworth's diary is the son of Captain Davidson.

The potential correlation of Old Mrs. Davidson—the mother of John Hughes's wife, Nancy—to the same widow Davidson, whose husband died in the Revolutionary War, was granted a western Pennsylvania Depreciation Tract and is the mother of a Joseph, Nancy, Mary and Nathan Davidson, is remarkable, albeit inferred. Especially considering the Joseph Davidson and McCaskey family association corroborated by Reverend Dilworth's Diary.

It is also unclear why this Depreciation land request was made so long after the war. If Lydia Davidson were John Hughes's mother-in-law, she would have died a few weeks before Joseph Davidson's Depreciation land claim was filed. This timeline conflict is troubling; however, it is possible that Joseph had to refile his application more than once due to the widespread land disputes of the day.* Bausman's *History of Beaver County* describes in detail how property suits caused by conflicting land ownership claims by persons

---

* Another possible but unproven reason could be that Lydia would not file because her husband was missing in action and she refused to accept his probable death as a prisoner of war.

who purchased the property from the state, those claiming title under the 1792 clause of "settlement and improvement" and by lands granted under depreciation certificates tied up the court system for over forty years.[44] This very issue was the core of Beaver County's first murder trial mentioned earlier. The fact that the Davidson Depreciation claim was granted on June 6, 1827, within two weeks of Joseph Davidson filing the request, supports this theory.[45]

It's also possible that the circumstances of Captain Davidson's demise confounded his family's land claim. According to the Revolutionary War Pension and Bounty Land Warrant Application filed by Joseph on behalf of his deceased father, Captain Davidson was never heard from again after being taken as a prisoner of war.[46] The Davidson family likely had to wade through the postwar red tape of a newly forming nation to prove their father's death in service to his country.

Another piece of anecdotal evidence confounds this mystery even further. In a somewhat unremarkable essay, Mansfield describes the historical importance of Christ Church in Philadelphia, which he attended as a child until the age of eight.[47] Mansfield's father moved his family to Philadelphia shortly after his birth. Although he visited relatives on occasion, Mansfield didn't relocate to Poland, Ohio, until after the passing of his father in 1850. It may be purely circumstantial, but Ira attended this church when a prosperous seventy-year-old Philadelphia businessman died and was laid to rest in the Christ Churchyard in 1849. That man's name was Nathan Davidson. Davidson being such a common name, I am unable to determine if this is the same Nathan whose brother filed for a western Pennsylvania Depreciation tract; however, joining him in his family vault is a son named William. Might this Nathan have named his son after his father, Captain William Davidson? Was he in Beaver County, scouting Depreciation tracts for or with his brother Joseph before returning to Philadelphia? If so, as an elderly man did Nathan Davidson relate tales of early Beaver County to little Ira Mansfield, a youth in his Christ Church congregation whose uncle had purchased coal mines and began building a railroad in his old stomping grounds? At the time of writing (in analytic writing, this is called the information cutoff date), I lack the necessary data to formulate objective judgments regarding these gaps of information, however it is interesting that this Nathan Davidson was born very near the same time as Barbara, according to Mr. Oswald's version of the story.

Nathan Davidson is a common name, but I can find no record of someone with it in the Revolutionary War records from Virginia, as claimed by Mr.

Nathan Davidson's grave marker, Christ Church, Philadelphia. *www.findagrave.com.*

Oswald. A private named Nathan Davidson did serve in the Twenty-Third Virginia Regiment during the War of 1812. It is almost certain that this Nathan Davidson and the one who later attended Christ Church in Philadelphia are not the same person. In 1812, the latter Nathan would have been a suitable age (thirty-three) but records show that private Davidson of the Twenty-Third Virginia Regiment later drew a pension while living in the state of Louisiana, which is about as far away as one could get from Pennsylvania within the borders of the United States at the time.[48]

One final note from a supplementary source: it appears that Mr. Mansfield's reporting of the 1849 eviction of Samuel McCaskey from his Cannelton settlement cabin is at least somewhat accurate. The 1850 Darlington Township census lists Samuel as being a fifty-eight-year-old tenant of the forty-year-old widow Best and her three children.[49] Widow Best married Samuel, becoming Mary McCaskey. The two would move to Illinois according to census data, having two more children intriguingly named Nancy and Mary.

## Assumptions, Knowns, Unknowns and Theories

Once you've established viable hypotheses with a modicum of credibility, policymakers want to know three things from intelligence officers: what you know, what you don't know and what you think. To maintain integrity, a respectable analyst will state assumptions up front. At this point, we can hypothesize that Barbara Davidson existed, but whether or not her murder occurred is up for debate.

## *Knowns from Official Sources*

William (born 1791) and Samuel McCaskey (born 1792) lived in the Little Beaver River Valley.

- Both were born in Pennsylvania according to census data.
- The earliest record the author located for a McCaskey in Beaver County is a land warrant for William tying him to his Little Beaver Township property in 1807.*
- Samuel is probably not Barbara's father, as claimed by Oswald, based on his birth date.
- Mansfield never claims that Samuel is Barbara's father and suggests that her murder happens sometime after 1799.
- William McCaskey was well acquainted with John Hughes, owner of the land on which Barbara Davidson's alleged homicide took place, and on which Samuel lives until 1849. A series of diary entries discloses William McCaskey and Joseph Davidson's children were stricken with scarlet fever, suggesting their families were either related or at least very close. Joseph lost three children to the disease.
- John Hughes's mother-in-law, old Mrs. Davidson, died in 1827.
- John Hughes was married to Nancy Davidson.
- A Joseph Davidson from Philadelphia, son of Captain William Davidson, who died serving in the Revolution, was granted a three-hundred-acre Depreciation tract in western Pennsylvania in 1827.
- The claim was filed on behalf of all of Captain Davidson's descendants to include his wife, Lydia, sons Joseph and Nathan and daughters Lydia, Mary, Sarah and Nancy.
- The claim was eventually granted at an extraordinary late date considering the war ended in 1783, suggesting the land claim was disputed, as was commonplace in Beaver County at the time.

---

* Darlington Township, where Cannelton is located, was split away from Little Beaver Township in 1846.

## *Unknowns*

Motives are not apparent, and according to the story the only persons with alibis appear to be immediate family. It is unknown

- Whether or not Samuel is the younger brother of William or if Barbara is their sister.
- When the McCaskeys actually arrived in Beaver County, Pennsylvania.
- If Samuel and his cohorts were counterfeiters and thieves as claimed by Ira Mansfield.
- Whether or not Mary McCaskey or Mary Davidson was Barbara's sister-in-law.
- Whether or not Joseph and Nancy Davison living in the Little Beaver River Valley are the same heirs of Captain William Davidson who finally successfully claimed a three-hundred-acre Revolutionary War Depreciation tract in 1827.
- Whether or not their brother Nathan was once Barbara's husband.
- Or whether or not this is the Nathan Davidson who was a member of the same Christ Church congregation Ira Mansfield was a member of in his youth.
- Whether or not Barbara's husband was the Nathan Davidson who was a veteran of the War of 1812, serving in the Twenty-Third Virginia Regiment.
- When or why Barbara and her husband separated.
- Whether or not Mary Davidson later became Mary Ragan.
- Whether or not Lydia Davidson was John Hughes's mother-in-law who died in Beaver County, Pennsylvania, in 1827.
- Whether or not John Hughes's mother-in-law was Barbara Davidson.
- Whether or not Barbara McCaskey-Davidson ever existed.

Even without sufficient primary evidence, we can extract enough substance from the stories and historical record to form a few hypotheses. For the sake of argument, let's assume three essential details occurred: Barbara McCaskey was the sister of Samuel, an outlaw of some sort; Barbara's family was away when she is beheaded during Cannelton's pioneer era; and her killer got away.

## Theory 1. Life and Crime on the Frontier

It's well documented that before Tombstone or Dodge City existed, the wild west of the Revolutionary War period ran along the Ohio River. As noted in Bausman's history of the county, "Among the pioneer settlers were many of the worst elements of the old-world population; men who were deported here for their crimes, and who brought with them their criminal instincts and practices."[50] While Mansfield's references to Samuel McCaskey as a counterfeiter and thief do not supply a direct cause for Barbara's murder, it offers a reason to question whether or not her unfortunate demise is a result of her relative's unlawful dealings. Both crimes were felonies, as horse theft was akin to grand theft auto at the time.

## Theory 2. Geography and Terrorism

Beginning with Pontiac's Rebellion in 1763 through the signing of the Treaty of Greenville in 1795, several Native American tribes fought European settlers for control of the Ohio Valley. Increasingly reduced by European diseases like smallpox, the tribes turned to asymmetric warfare tactics early in the conflict, hoping fear would stave off the tide of immigrants. Kidnapping, scalping and torture were common forms of terrorism that proved successful (albeit temporarily), particularly after major U.S. military defeats in 1790 and 1791. In 1791, Major John Irwin of the Pennsylvania militia wrote, "We are perfectly easy on the subject of tomahawking and scalping, as it happens every two or three days. It is probable I may not have the pleasure of writing you again, as I believe mine [his scalp] would be very acceptable to our swarthy neighbors."[51] Attacks on Ohio settlers didn't stop after the Greenville treaty, but they were less organized. A major factor causing the natives to sign the agreement was the loss of British support. Indians still populated much of northwestern Ohio for several decades. Leading up to and during the War of 1812, these tribes regained British backing and formed another powerful confederacy of native nations under Tecumseh. Ohioans weren't entirely safe from Indian attack until his death in 1813. Language in the Treaty of Ghent, which ended the war, specified that the British would stop arming Native Americans in the United States from Canada.

Might Barbara have fallen victim to an Indian attack while her family was away? It is doubtful, but depending on the date of the actual murder, this is a possibility considering Cannelton's location in the zone of conflict.

Members of the Wyandot tribe who captured and assimilated George Foulks would visit him into the 1820s to trade furs for whiskey and other goods.[52] According to Mansfield, some would stay in the empty cabin once owned by John Bridgeman on the same tract of land as the McCaskeys.[53] Warriors from this tribe didn't hesitate to kill George's older brother John, his stepbrother and three neighbor boys during the raid in which he and his sister were taken captive.[54] Unfortunately, the practice of beheading victims was not new to the long struggle. A horrific warning was observed near what is now the Seven Oaks Country Club in Brighton Township, during Colonel Bouquet's 1764 expedition. An entry in his orderly book states, "Two miles beyond Beaver-creek, by two small springs, was seen the skull of a child that had been fixed on a pole by Indians."[55]

## *Theory 3. Jilted Love*

Both versions of Barbara's story indicate she had competing suitors. Jealousy and infidelity are a primary cause of domestic violence today, and there is no reason to suspect it wouldn't have been an equally common motivation in the eighteenth century.

## *Theory 4. PTSD*

An unfortunate reality, post-traumatic stress disorder is a common affliction of combat veterans. However, violence is not a typical symptom unless coupled with alcohol abuse. Untreated, the likelihood of domestic violence increases 35 percent in that situation according to an article in the *British Journal of Psychiatry*.[56] If Barbara married a military veteran of the Revolution, Northwest Indian War or the War of 1812, he most likely served in a conflict zone and might have suffered from this condition.

Usually, the next step of the analytic process would be to conduct a structured analytic technique such as an analysis of competing hypotheses to determine which theory is most likely.* This works if the intelligence is plausible, but in the case of folklore we can assume some data points are fanciful, so I chose not to undertake the effort.

---

* Analysis of competing hypotheses, sometimes abbreviated ACH, is a tool to aid judgment on important issues requiring careful weighing of alternative explanations or conclusions. It helps an analyst overcome, or at least minimize, some of the cognitive limitations that make prescient intelligence analysis so difficult to achieve.

## PORCINE POSTSCRIPT

None of the evidence collected explains the apparent contemporary modification of Barbara's story incorporating a replacement pig head. Rich Oswald revealed in an interview for Thomas White's book that he believed this part of the legend probably emerged in the twentieth century as teenagers went looking for the ghost.[57] He's probably not wrong. The phenomenon is more common than you might expect.

Pig-faced phantoms and pig-faced lady myths have endured for quite some time. Buddhist scriptures tell of a foul-tongued brother tortured for his sins in hell, who, through the ripening of his karma, came to life as a ghost with a pig's face.[58] Another spirit, this time a pig-faced lady, allegedly haunted a reverend and his family in London according to a story written in 1924.[59] Finally, the gothic mystery novel *Uncle Silas: A Tale of Bartram-Haugh* includes the following poem.[60]

> *This lady was neither pig nor maid,*
> *And so she was not of human mould;*
> *Not of the living nor the dead.*
> *Her left hand and foot were warm to touch;*
> *Her right as cold as a corpse's flesh!*
> *And she would sing like a funeral bell, with a ding-dong tune.*
> *The pigs were afraid, and viewed her aloof;*
> *And women feared her and stood afar.*
> *She could do without sleep for a year and a day;*
> *She could sleep like a corpse, for a month and more.*
> *No one knew how this lady fed—*
> *On acorns or on flesh.*
> *Some say that she's one of the swine-possessed,*
> *That swam over the sea of Gennesaret.*
> *A mongrel body and demon soul.*
> *Some say she's the wife of the Wandering Jew,*
> *And broke the law for the sake of pork;*
> *And a swinish face for a token doth bear,*
> *That her shame is now, and her punishment coming.*

Pig Lady ghost legends also exist in Elkton, Maryland, and Hillsborough, New Jersey.[61] Though not as intricate as Barbara's story, both involve a menacing ghost of a woman with a pig for a head who attacks teenagers at night, sometimes with an axe. Although I cannot find a conclusive link to these stories, it's easy to imagine how the legend of Barbara Davidson could blend with the Pig Lady urban myth over time.[62]

3

# ESTHER HALE

## AN OHIO GHOST TOWN'S LADY IN WHITE

A nother tale that seems to have deviated wildly since Mansfield's day is the legend of Esther Hale. Esther is far more famous in death than in life, having dozens of references to her apparition in books, websites, a country western song and even as the antagonist in a low-budget horror movie. A quick YouTube search reveals a surprising number of ghost hunter videos documenting both some strange findings and plenty of what I assume to be harmless but criminal breaking and entering into state park property.

Esther's story takes place in the ghost town of Sprucevale, Ohio, along the western fork of the Little Beaver Creek—allegedly populated with more ghosts than buildings. Now part of the Little Beaver Creek State Park, the village was organized along the Sandy and Beaver Canal route in 1835 by the Hambleton brothers according to an excellent history of the canal's construction written by R. Max Gard:

> *The town was a busy place in those days. James Hambleton was a director of the Canal Company and ran the grist mill, Charles kept the store and post office, Isaac ran the woolen factory, and Benjamin remained on the family farm. There being no more brothers, Samson Risinger was the village blacksmith, fulfilling the fond hopes of his parents when they named him. He was succeeded by William Supplee. The woolen factory for a time had William Davidson as a partner; while later grist millers were George West and William Dougherty.*

Evidence of breaking and entering at Hambleton's Mill.

> *There was also a flax seed oil mill founded by Brookes and the usual sawmill. The water power for all the industries was furnished by the canal dam. Other canal structures were two locks and a warehouse. Twelve to fifteen families were supported by the work of the village. The village never had a church or school. The Hambleton's were members of the Hicksite Quaker meeting at East Carmel, two miles north of Clarkson.*[63]

Today, the remaining bits of Sprucevale include the ruins of the two canal locks, a few building foundations and the external shell of the gristmill. I suspect Hale's myth benefitted from the horror revival of the 1990s, as although I was well aware of the haunted lock known as Gretchen's (more on this later), I didn't know Esther's story growing up. I first read about her in the well-liked Weird U.S. series of books. This clever anthology is masterful in its simplicity, oozing with vivid imagery and stories told in the rural tongue typical of any rustic campground. But for all the delightful representation, the series, like most folklore collections, is frustratingly devoid of source citation.

The synopsis of Esther's story in *Weird Ohio* shadows the majority of those I've managed to find in other books and websites.[64] In short, Esther, living in Sprucevale in the early 1800s, gleefully prepares for an August wedding that never occurs, as her unnamed groom fails to arrive for the ceremony. Grief-struck to the point of desperate insanity, the jilted bride spends the next several months in her cabin refusing to leave until one particularly harsh winter day when a passerby noticed snow drifting against her open cabin door. Further inspection reveals her corpse still clad in a wedding dress, apparently having succumbed to starvation. Some accounts suggest her husband never returned from the Civil War.[65] Other books, such as *Haunted Ohio II: More Ghostly Tales from the Buckeye State*, set the wedding date much earlier, specifically on August 12, 1837.[66] Most claim she haunts a bridge over the creek—still clad in her wedding attire, harassing cars as they pass. If she manages to touch a living person, she steals their life force, becoming young again as her victims shrivel and die. *Weird Ohio* and *Haunted Ohio II* disagree on when one should look for Esther to materialize. The first claims she is particularly active and dangerous on the anniversary of her planned August 12 nuptials, while the latter suggests she is liveliest on Christmas Eve.

Bridge over the Little Beaver at Sprucevale.

## Analysis of Evidence: Source Derivation

At first glance, this story could quickly be written off as suspect because it depicts nearly all the classic components of the traditional Lady in White folktale. Even more widespread than the crybaby bridge fable, it seems as if almost every state in the Union along with many European countries have versions of the White Lady fable. This legend might be the most pervasive ghost story in the world. The phantom female is nearly always clad in white (usually a wedding dress), symbolizing the girl's innocence. She is frequently associated with a body of water—sometimes it causes her death. Also standard is the causation of her existence, a drive to obtain justice or revenge for some emotional injury or worse, her murder.[67]

The Esther Hale legend was probably widespread in Mansfield's time, as he never fully divulges the entire plot, seemingly content in the story being so well known that specifics were not necessary to preserve in his books. Although the amount of detail Mansfield provides is small, it reveals distinct differences between the story then and now. First, Ira Mansfield's hundred-plus-year-old version mentions nothing about a wedding, the August 12 date, Christmas Eve or Esther haunting a bridge. Mansfield claims, "In the

Hambleton's Mill.

deserted stone mill at Sprucevale, on St. Nicholas Eve, the ghost of Esther Hale, the Quaker Lady preacher, appears and rewrites on the stone wall in her old text 'Come.'"[68] He mentions her spirit again in a later text by simply describing Sprucevale as the place where "little Gretchen's cache and stone mill where Esther Hale, still in visions appears each year."[69]

## ANALYSIS OF EVIDENCE: SUPPLEMENTAL SOURCES

St. Nicholas Eve is the night before the Feast of St. Nicholas, a holiday celebrating the patron saint of children on December 6. No longer popular in Western religions, some of the old traditions associated with this holiday—such as leaving out shoes and stockings to be filled with treats and presents—have melded with Christmas, possibly explaining why some versions of Esther's story claim her spirit is more active on Christmas Eve.

Still standing in Beaver Creek State Park, Hambleton's gristmill is the structure that is often broken into by paranormal investigators searching for evidence of Esther's ethereal existence. Interestingly, in two years of gathering pictures for this book, the only photographic abnormality I recorded occurred at this location. It didn't appear until I attempted to upload a photo of the mill's interior to a Pig Lady fan site. Facebook's facial recognition software, used for auto-tagging user accounts to photos, identified an unseen face. Multiple attempts to reload the picture provided the same result. The anomaly did not appear in other images that I took or in ones my sister logged from the same location. For the record, I make no claims regarding the cause of the anomaly—only that it occurred—and hasn't happened in hundreds of other photos I've uploaded using the same software. Also, for the record, the photo was taken from outside the structure, through the bars of a closed entrance. Mansfield elucidates no further on Esther as a specter but does discuss her life as a Quaker in a separate essay about local churches.

> *The Carmel church of the Orthodox Friends was organized in Middleton township about 1810. They held monthly meetings, and yet their ministers only preached as moved by the Holy Spirit. Among their first ministers was Esther Hale, an earnest worker who labored many years among the workmen on the Sandy and Beaver canal. Many of the early settlers have kindly remembrances of her good work.*[70]

This point is corroborated by the 1891 *History of the Upper Ohio Valley*, which chronicled early Columbiana County, Ohio residents and events. This text notes important details left absent in Mansfield's description. Most significantly it substantiates Esther's tie to the mill, or at least its operator, James Hambleton.

> *The Carmel meeting of the Orthodox Friends was organized in Middleton about 1810. The first year a log meeting house was built on a lot donated by Jacob Heacock and was used until 1835 when the new one was built and partially destroyed by fire in 1845. The first monthly meeting at Carmel was on December 12, 1817. Joseph Fisher and Nathan Heald were the first clerks. Nathan Hale, Abijah Richards, and Esther Hale were the first ministers. The monthly meetings discontinued in the fall of 1854, nearly all the old members having died or removed. The Friends living in that neighborhood, however, held monthly meetings at Middleton after that date, and on September 29 1828, a number of Friends who had been accused by the regular meeting of defection of doctrine assembled at Elk Run, and appointed James Hambleton clerk; and Eli Vale, James Marsh and Thomas McMillen to confer as to what future action should be taken. They reported that they thought that the harmony of the society would be promoted if those holding the belief of Friend Hicks would hold a meeting separate from our accusing brethren, and for this purpose a house was proffered by Jesse Underwood for the time, and James Hambleton, Jacob Heacock, and Benjamin Pyle were appointed to make arrangements with the opposing party for the use of the meeting house. Accordingly, on December 20, 1828, Jacob Heacock and Benjamin Pyle were appointed overseers of the meeting, which was permanently organized with James Hambleton as a clerk and Thomas McMillen assistant. At a later session James Hambleton, John Edmundson and Jacob Heacock were appointed to build a meeting house which was accordingly erected in 1829. Until about 1845 the meetings were well attended, but at this time many of the members removed that after December 1851 no monthly meetings were held. The Carmel monthly meeting for women was established in 1820 but discontinued in 1840.*[71]

An amateur historian of note, Ira Mansfield maintained a personal library of historical texts that he almost certainly used as source material in authoring his books. The nearly identical language he used in describing the Carmel Meeting of the Orthodox Friends shows that he probably had access to a copy of *History of the Upper Ohio Valley*, which is an essential piece of evidence I'll reference shortly.

Esther's tie to Hicksite Quaker mill operator James Hambleton links her to Sprucevale. The 1820s Orthodox Quaker reformation, which limited the roles of women in the church, would affect Esther's position as a Quaker minister. As the passage alluded, a group within the Carmel Orthodox Friends headed by James Hambleton left the church following the Hicks-Orthodox split of 1828. Female "Hicksites" retained equal influence in this progressive sect of Quakerism, whereas Orthodox Quakers began separating men and women for both business and worship, as indicated by the establishment of a separate Carmel monthly meeting for women in 1820.

> ALSO, IN 1817
> *The four-year torment of the Bell family of Adams, Tennessee, by Old Kate Batt's witch began in late autumn of 1817. The Bell Witch account describes poltergeist or demonic activity rather than traditional witchcraft, inspiring the popular movie* The Blair Witch Project.

Locating further data on Esther Hale proved to be abnormally tricky. I expected that accounts of her ministry would be readily available. Quaker meetings, as their congregations are called, keep thorough records, each having a clerk. A more in-depth look at the Orthodox Society at Carmel revealed that Esther's last name was not Hale. A typographical error in *History of the Upper Ohio Valley* perpetuated later by Mansfield might be the causative reason for the lack of plot details in Mansfield's version of Esther's story. The 1879 *History of Columbiana County* includes a near word-for-word copy of the Carmel meeting of the Orthodox Friends description published twelve years later in *History of the Upper Ohio Valley*, except for one minor detail. In the earlier account, Esther's last name is Hole.[72] Much information is available about Esther Hanna Hole, her interesting, affluent family and her ties to the Sandy and Beaver Canal.

Esther Hanna married Charles Hole on May 16, 1811, in Middleton Township, Ohio, and together they had eleven children.[73] Esther passed away on the Feast of Saint Nicholas (December 6) in 1849 at the age of fifty-eight. She died in Clarkson, Ohio, a village her father founded very near Sprucevale. Her obituary in *Friends Review*, an early Quaker journal, states that Esther remained a minister and member of the Carmel meeting of the Society of Friends her entire life.[74] Esther was an ardent abolitionist, preaching against the evils of slavery throughout Ohio and Virginia.[75] Both a minister and an abolitionist before the women's rights movement began in earnest, Esther almost certainly would be disappointed in her portrayal

Benjamin Hanna. *From Gard and Vodrey,* The Sandy and Beaver Canal.

today as a weak-minded youth so unable to cope with male rejection that her melancholy literally and figuratively destroys her.

Before arriving in Ohio, Esther's father, Robert Hanna, partnered with John Lynch in founding Lynchburg, Virginia. Before that, he was reportedly a member of the committee that met at Carpenter's Hall in Philadelphia in July 1774 to draft a resolution calling for delegates to attend the first Continental Congress. President James Monroe purportedly visited Esther's mother, Catherine, in Ohio. President Monroe was Catherine's first cousin.[76]

Whether or not the rift in the Quaker society affected Esther's ability to minister to the Hicksite Hambletons after they were asked to leave the church, she had reason to continue to visit Sprucevale after 1828. Esther's brother, Benjamin Hanna was the president of the Sandy and Beaver Canal Company for twenty-five years, while her sister Ann married Benjamin Hambleton of Sprucevale in 1815.[77] Recall that James Hambleton, the mill operator and a director in the Sandy and Beaver Canal Company, was Benjamin Hambleton's brother.

I failed to find a definitive reason for Esther's ghost to scrawl the word *come* on the Hambleton Mill walls each December 5. It's probable that "come" is a reference to the popular George Fox quote often cited by Quakers, "Christ has come to teach his people himself." George Fox founded the Quaker Society of Religious Friends. The quote is meant to emphasize a direct relationship to God through Jesus rather than through man, as in priests in Catholicism or the Anglican Church. Being a female minister before and during the Quaker orthodox reformation, which limited female equality in the church, may have strengthened the importance of this quotation to her. It's possible Mansfield is suggesting that Esther's apparition appears in the mill operated by her congregation's lead Hicksite defector, to scroll a message portraying her regret for not joining him in the Quaker progressive movement.

Conversely, Mansfield could simply be suggesting Esther haunts the Hambletons for betraying her. In fact, the Orthodox/Hicksite split affected Esther deeply. Her mother, Catherine Hanna, sister Ann Hambleton and brother Benjamin Hanna were among those accused by her orthodox sect

Interior wall at Hambleton's Mill (taken from outside).

of defecting from church doctrine.[78] Being a church elder and minister, this caused her great consternation. In a letter dated May 5, 1828, to another sister, Catherine Hole,* who was an elder in the Augusta Meeting of Friends (also Orthodox) in Carroll County, Ohio, Esther decries:

> *I may inform thee, that my trials have been great respecting the state of our society and the alarming division that is taking place among Friends, but stand still and seek the salvation of our God, for he is the same always. He was and will be a strong tower to those that put their trust in him. For my part, I cannot see what is to be gained by departing from the society. Indeed, it appears to be a delusion of the adversary of our peace.*[79]

## Assumptions, Knowns, Unknowns and Theories

This one is relatively cut and dried. Esther Hale, the lovesick bride, left at the altar, never existed. A look at the knowns and unknowns involved rendered only one viable alternative theory.

---

* Sisters Esther and Catherine Hanna married brothers Charles and John Hole.

## *Knowns*

- Esther Hale was actually Esther Hole.
- She was a minister in the Orthodox Meeting of Friends at Carmel, Ohio.
- She married and had eleven children.
- Her brother was the president of the Sandy and Beaver Canal Company.
- The Hambleton brothers, one of whom was her brother-in-law, founded Sprucevale as a canal town on the Sandy and Beaver route.
- The Hambletons also were members of Esther's congregation.
- James Hambleton, mill operator and a director in the Sandy and Beaver Canal Company, led the defection of several parishioners (to include her mother, sister and brother) from her ministry.*
- Esther died on the Feast of Saint Nicholas (St. Nicholas Day) in 1849.

## *Unknowns*

- Why Esther's story metamorphosed into a Lady in White legend and when?
- How much the religious rift affected Esther, her family and friends?
- Why the implication exists that her alleged ghost haunts the abandoned mill in Sprucevale, writing "Come" on the wall each December 5?
- If Ira Mansfield chose to align Esther's death with St. Nicholas Eve out of coincidence, the date of her death, or he attempted to find meaning in her stature as a Quaker minister with the holiday? The latter seems less likely considering Orthodox Quaker views regarding the observance of religious celebrations at the time.

---

* Fun fact—William Foulks also lived in Sprucevale for a while after leaving Cannelton and almost certainly knew Esther. William was Charlie Foulks's (early Robin Hood Club member) father. As discussed earlier, Charlie liked to tell stories about the ghost of Barbara Davidson.

## *Theory: Mid-Nineteenth-Century Religion and Feminism*

Although today's most popular version of Esther's story as a lovesick recluse isn't a defendable theory, Mansfield's version of a ghostly preacher is still viable assuming a belief in the supernatural. Instead of the White Lady legend associated with Esther today, might her alleged haunting of the Hambleton Mill be a representation of her continued struggle in the afterlife to reconcile the church congregation she devoted her life to caring for? It couldn't have been easy to choose faith over family. I assume Mansfield's full Esther Hale story may have been the tale of an early abolitionist conflicted by her feelings about women's rights versus religious and familial responsibility. This story would have captivated members of his second Robin Hood Club who were heavily involved in the women's suffrage movement at the time—particularly if he wove in historical details such as the first American women's rights convention held during Esther's time in 1848. Convened at Seneca Falls, New York, the gathering was organized by Quaker women.

# 4

# GRETCHEN'S LOCK

This next tale, centered just a short walk from the Hambleton Mill, is atypical to regional fables, which often focus on nondescript characters about which little backstory is available. The protagonist, Gretchen, is said to be the daughter of a notable civil engineer about whom plenty is on record for posterity. Gretchen is one of the most famed of Sprucevale's many ghosts, showing up in dozens of books and at least one movie. Unlike the Pig Lady or Esther Hale, the integrity of this folktale is well preserved, as for the most part little has changed from the version Mansfield recorded over one hundred years ago.*

> *There is a sad and touching legend of E.H. Gill, the chief civil engineer. He was a graduate of the Royal Engineer's School at Paris, France. On the ocean voyage across to America, his wife was washed overboard and drowned. Their little seven-year-old daughter living with the father in the camps along the Little Beaver was taken sick with fever and died. Before her death, she exacted a promise from her father to take her home and bury her with her mother. Little Gretchen was temporarily placed in a stone cache in Lock No. 41, just above Spruce Vale. On completion of the canal E.H. Gill, with the remains of his daughter, took a ship from Baltimore*

---

* One notable exception being Gretchen's story is completely reimagined by author Ran Cartwright as a demonic fishlike beast created by Mr. Gill that needed to feed on a sacrificial volunteer once a month or it would destroy Spucevale. The beast's first victim was Esther Hale's fiancée, driving her insane.

Gretchen's Lock interior.

> *for France. In a severe storm near the Madeira Islands, the ship foundered, and all on board were lost. Thus, was little Gretchen's request realized and she was "buried with her mother."*[80]

## Analysis of Evidence: Source Derivation

In an article about the Little Beaver ghost that includes mentions of Barbara Davidson and Esther Hale, Mansfield claims, "At the canal lock below Vondergreen's, little Gretchen has often appeared murmuring her dying prayer 'bury me with my mother.'"[81] Mansfield professed that his version of the story came from a seemingly credible primary source.

> *On our first visit to the handsome old Sandy and Beaver lock in 1866, two miles below Elkton, we met the old sub-contractor Scotch Campbell, who had helped cut the stone and erect the double pair of winding steps to this canal lock. He related many incidents of the old canal, and the tragic and*

Lusk Lock winding stairs.

> *touching loss of the chief engineer's wife on the ocean; the death of little Gretchen, with her request to be "buried with my mother" and so tragically carried out by the loss of the ship on return to France.*

I failed to locate evidence of Scotch Campbell's affiliation with lock construction on the canal system. "Scotch" is likely a nickname, which undoubtedly complicated my research. Like Mansfield's association with Charley Foulks, his 1866 meeting with a potential Sandy and Beaver Canal stonemason lends higher authority to the story.

## Analysis of Evidence: Supplemental Sources

The celebrated East Liverpool historian R. Max Gard relates a nearly identical version in his 1952 book *The Sandy and Beaver Canal*. It's noteworthy that Gard later cites "Captain Mansfield" for copying and preserving Gill's map of the complete Sandy and Beaver Canal dam system in his *"Historical Collections of Beaver Creek."* Although not credited, Gard almost certainly borrowed directly from Mansfield's work in retelling Gretchen's story.

*According to legend, E.H. Gill with his wife and their beloved little daughter Gretchen started to America from Europe. On the trip to America, Gretchen's mother died and was buried at sea. The grief-stricken father and his little daughter Gretchen completed the journey. At the time, the lock was being constructed above Sprucevale, Gretchen contracted malaria and died. A crypt was prepared in the masonry of the lock and Gretchen was entombed in the lock for a while. When Gill resigned and decided to go back to Europe, Daughter Gretchen's casket was removed from the crypt in the lock and taken on board ship to be returned to her birthplace for burial. On the trip back, a storm came up at sea, and all aboard were lost. E.H. Gill and Gretchen joined their wife and mother in the waters of the Atlantic. Little Gretchen's monument is the lock near Sprucevale where she was entombed. Everyone who knows of this lock knows of it as "Gretchen's Lock." The pilgrims who wish to make the trip to see the lock will be rewarded with a view of the opened crypt where Gretchen slept for a while.*[82]

Gretchen's Lock entrance.

Gard undoubtedly read about the alleged haunting of the antiquated canal relic in Mansfield's book. The story is so prevalent today that the state park service erected a kiosk near the lock regaling a very similar version of the tale. The 2005 printing of *Weird Ohio* popularized the story nationally, with a few minor differences. First, the *Weird Ohio* adaptation claims Gill is either from Ireland or the Netherlands rather than France and that he was brought over explicitly to work on the Sandy and Beaver Canal system. Second, like Gard's version, *Weird Ohio* claims Gill's wife became sick and died onboard the ship, rather than being swept overboard. Finally, it professes,

> *It would appear that Gretchen finally got her wish to be reunited with her mother…in a watery grave. The girl's body was never seen again. But in a strange twist, Gretchen's ghost has been spotted wandering near the lock in which her body was temporarily entombed, often on the anniversary of her death, August 12. As she moves along the lock, Gretchen is said to be weeping and can be heard crying out, "I want to be with my mother."*[83]

On top of Gretchen's Lock.

Several other mostly online accounts claim Gretchen died on August 12, often in the year 1837 or '38, probably conflating her story with Esther Hale's. Nearly all cite malaria as the cause of death.

ALSO, IN 1837
*Spring-heeled Jack allegedly attacks his first victim in England. His reign of terror would reportedly last more than four decades, without ever being caught.*

Proof of E.H. Gill's association to the Sandy and Beaver Canal is well documented and irrefutable. Gill was the chief engineer of the canal system for a little over three years, from June 1834 until he resigned during the economic panic of 1837, filing his last annual report to the company on August 7 of that year.[84] Gretchen Gill couldn't have died in Sprucevale while Gill worked on the lock named for her in 1838 because he'd already left by then. Much like the housing market crash of 2007, speculative lending practices and a collapsing real estate bubble led to a significant and long-lasting recession beginning in 1837. Beyond upkeep, major work on the canal ground to a halt until 1845.[85]

Available evidence proves Gill did not remove the corpse of his daughter from a lock in Sprucevale and then perish by drowning in route to Europe

Gill's plaque on Lusk Lock.

Masonic carving on Lusk Lock.

E.H. Gill's headstone.

with it. After leaving work on the Sandy and Beaver, Gill was hired to build canals for the James River and Kanawha Company in Virginia in 1838.[86] In Virginia, he was both a mason by trade and by fraternal order. Gill was grand commander of the Masonic order of the Knights Templar of Virginia for many years, including those that spanned the Civil War.[87] Masonic Royal Arch Chapter no. 50 in Abington, Virginia, carries his name in tribute. He lived out his remaining years in the South working as a civil engineer developing both canal and railroad systems.[88] Edward H. Gill died in Richmond, Virginia, on December 20, 1868, and is buried with his wife, Mary, in Richmond's Hollywood Cemetery. I found no evidence to suggest that Gill had a previous marriage, lowering the possibility that Gretchen's mother died at sea.

## Analysis of Evidence: The Timeline

According to an online chronology of undetermined reliability, E.H. Gill was born in Ireland and emigrated with his father (also an engineer) at or before the age of thirteen, calling into question claims that he married and had a child before arriving in America.[89] The chronology is unsourced, but several points noted within are verifiable in census data, Gard's book and the Library of Congress, conferring some credibility.* A report authored by Gill detailing his work on the Schuylkill Canal, work which he completed two months before being hired as the chief engineer of the Sandy and Beaver Canal Company, proves he was not brought from Europe expressly to work on the Sandy and Beaver. The report was republished later in a book Gill coauthored four years after his supposed death at sea.[90]

## Assumptions, Knowns, Unknowns and Theories

A strong assessment regarding the authenticity of this tale is easy to ascertain by outlining knowns and unknowns derived from available sources. Determining the driving motivation behind the story's

---

* E.H. Gill published reports of his engineering projects in Ohio, Pennsylvania, Georgia and Virginia. Many are preserved today in archive.org and the Library of Congress. Additionally, U.S. Census data from 1850 and 1860 indicates he resided in Campbell County, Virginia, with his wife, Mary.

development is more challenging, but I am confident that the theory I devised and discuss later in the Conclusions chapter is sound.

## *Knowns*

- E.H. Gill was chief engineer for the Sandy and Beaver Canal Company from June 1834 until August 1837.
- Following his resignation from the Sandy and Beaver Canal Company, Gill was hired by the James River and Kanawha Company in 1838.
- Gill remained in Virginia until his death in 1868.
- He did not die at sea while returning to Europe.
- Mary Gill, Edward's wife, also died in Virginia.
- Before working on the Sandy and Beaver Canal, Gill was employed as an engineer working on the Schuylkill Canal, proving he was not brought from Europe to work on the Sandy and Beaver Canal system.

## *Unknowns*

- Did Gretchen Gill ever exist?
- Was Mary Gill Edward's first wife?
- Was anyone entombed in Sandy and Beaver Canal lock number 41?

It's rare, but occasionally when conducting analysis, the evidence is so credible that formulating alternatives becomes unnecessary. I found no evidence of Gill having a daughter named Gretchen. Likewise, I am unsure if Mary was his first wife or if they had children. It appears that the integrity of this legend withstood the test of time without suffering heavy modification like Esther Hole's or Barbara Davidson's; however, unlike those central characters, Gretchen is likely a complete fabrication.

# 5
# THE FENNELL HOUSE AND OTHER LESSER KNOWN LITTLE BEAVER LEGENDS

## SPRUCEVALE

Several phantoms reportedly accompany Esther and Gretchen in Sprucevale, but Ira Mansfield makes no mention of them. This, coupled with my research failing to locate a shred of verifiable material to substantiate each story's origin (except for one infamous criminal), suggests they are entirely contrived. When Mansfield first visited Sprucevale in 1866, the community was already in its death throes, becoming abandoned by 1870. The failure of the Cold Run Reservoir Dam in 1852 put an end to canal operations. Many canal towns like Sprucevale were financially dependent on the Sandy and Beaver system and underwent a gradual abandonment. Sprucevale eventually became a favored camping site for groups like Mansfield's Robin Hood Club, and the scenic location continues to attract nature seekers as part of the Beaver Creek State Park today. Chances are these stories developed around a warm fire after days spent hiking the old canal towpath and exploring vacant buildings.

## JAKE'S LOCK

*Weird Ohio* includes the legend of Jake's Lock, which sits across a field from Hambleton's mill. A lockkeeper while the canal was still in operation, Jake

Jake's Lock.

was responsible for upkeep on Sprucevale's section of the system. One night, while he was inspecting that lock for damage during a thunderstorm, the lock was hit by lightning, killing Jake instantly. *Weird Ohio*'s authors claim campers often see Jake's lantern at night as he continues his ghostly rounds near the lock.[91] An email published in the book further insinuates that on at least one occasion, the spectral form of Esther clad in her wedding attire was observed holding a lantern and screaming for Jake, insinuating that he was that man who left her at the altar.

## THE LITTLE BOY

The shell of an abandoned brick building was haunted by an unnamed little boy according to deadohio.com, a website created to "document Northeast Ohio's haunted places, abandoned cemeteries, folklore and other oddities."[92] The boy allegedly hanged himself from the rafters. The Little Boy is the least-famous Sprucevale ghost story, as details are scarce and sources I found are entirely internet-based. Some say his name was David, but the reason for his suicide isn't apparent in the few accounts I could find. The park service demolished the building in 2007.

## PUBLIC ENEMY NUMBER ONE

Another book written by one of the authors of *Weird Ohio* claims Pretty Boy Floyd haunts the park and can be seen on October 22, the anniversary of his death.[93] He is observed most often on Sprucevale Road near the still open field on which he was gunned down, according to the book. Being such a widely publicized event both for the manner in which he died and it ending Floyd's infamous crime spree, plenty of primary sources are available to verify this story's origin. Charles Author Floyd, the FBI's public enemy number one, died on Sprucevale Road in 1934.[94]

Pretty Boy Floyd's appropriately bullet-riddled Ohio Historic Marker.

## The Mushroom Lady

One final Sprucevale legend described in small detail by Chris Woodyard, author of the popular *Haunted Ohio* series, is that of Lucy Cobb, Sprucevale's insane mushroom lady.[95] Dejected that a boy she loved had fallen for a prettier girl, Lucy poisoned the pair and buried them in her garden. Although I can find no primary or secondary sources to suggest she ever existed, Lucy is another popular spirit among the ghost-hunting community, having several EVPs (electronic voice phenomena) captured and posted to YouTube.

## Cannelton

Cannelton is the site of a couple of lesser-known hauntings as well. Oswald investigated them for a book that unfortunately never made it to publication before his passing. However, Rich's daughter graciously permitted me to include his versions of the tales in this chapter. Rather than summarizing the accounts, I'm adding the stories in their entirety, as Oswald's work is not readily available for follow-on researchers. The first details an exorcism that reportedly occurred in George Foulks's home long after his death.

### *The Fennell House Exorcism*

> *The house is gone now—demolished by a wrecking crew in 1991. Some locals say it was about time the local menace was gone. The Fennell House, as it came to be known by some of its more recent tenants, was constructed of local brick around the Civil War by B. Clayton. There were no stories of mysterious happenings in the house itself before the turn of the century until the terrible disaster in 1901 when the eight-member David Pfalph family decided to install gas lights, the latest technology, throughout the house. Unfortunately, the installation was done improperly, and during the first night, after the gas lines were activated, the whole family was asphyxiated. From then on, anyone who attempted to take up residence there began to report various phenomena such as sounds of people talking and laughing from inside the walls, steps on the stairways, strange flickering lights, levitated objects, and unidentified perfume-like smells. It did not help matters either that a small cemetery situated on a nearby knoll was the reported haunt of the decapitated woman, Barbara Davidson.*

The Fennell House. *Courtesy of the Little Beaver Historical Society.*

*Throughout the next fifty or so years many strange stories evolved around the supposed hauntings, but until 1948, there was nothing ever malicious about the happenings there other than what appeared to be the mischievous behavior of some of the local entities. It even seemed the atmosphere was friendly and warm with many of the residents acquiring a certain peace from regular nightly visitations. That changed in '48.*

*The house was inhabited at that time by two sisters, Margaret and Phyllis Fennell. As the story goes, neither of them were married. In fact, Margaret was considered somewhat challenged and that her sister Phyllis had dedicated her later life in her care. Phyllis, like others before her, had reported strange occurrences around the house, and her mentally disabled sister often claimed conversations with some of the spirits. Sometimes it seemed Margaret's only intelligent communication resulted from talks with her "friend" in the wall. The friend appeared harmless, but it was unfortunately discovered that was not the case.*

*It soon became apparent to her sister that Margaret was suddenly gaining weight—or else she was pregnant! Of course, that was impossible. Margaret was always around the house and Phyllis discouraged any visitors due to her sister's mental condition. Eventually, the impossible proved true.*

Margaret had somehow become pregnant even though Phyllis could not fathom any private visitations by a man in Margaret's second story bedroom. It was very difficult to get a straight answer from her sister. Every time she thought she was getting through to her, all Margaret said was the only man she knew was her friend in the wall!

That spring Margaret gave birth to a baby boy that she insisted be named Lucas after his father. In all respects, the child appeared healthy, and strangely, the mentally challenged girl was doing a credible job as its mother. That was—until one night about mid-July when Phyllis was awakened by terrible hysterical screaming. She rushed downstairs to the kitchen where the door to the stairway leading to the basement stood open. Margaret was standing at the head of the stairs swaying and moaning.

"He wanted Lucas! He wanted him! And I gave him Lucas!" "What did you do, Margaret? Tell me now," demanded Phyllis. Margaret pointed down the stairs. There, the infant lay—dead. Its head had been gruesomely smashed against the stones of the basement wall!

The police were called in that night, but no one could get anything but gibberish from Margaret. A month later, for her own good, Margaret was committed to an asylum near Pittsburgh. But for Phyllis, the nightmare lived on.

In her mind, every time she looked down the basement steps, she could visualize the blood on the wall. She thought she was going crazy. But then, when a few parishioners from the nearby church visited Phyllis to comfort her, they too claimed they saw, for a brief moment, the flash of gore on the stones. Later, others witnessing the spot for the first time, agreed they saw something as well. If that were not enough, regular wailing took place in the house, coming from the upper rooms. To make matters worse, the sound of a baby's mournful crying began to rise from the basement nightly—a cry that she immediately recognized as that of

### ALSO, IN 1948

The year 1948 was a busy one for the paranormal. On January 7, 1948, Kentucky Air National Guard pilot Captain Tom Mantell died while chasing a UFO. His P-51 Mustang crashed after climbing sharply to intercept the strange disk, with Tom probably succumbing to oxygen deprivation. A month later, the SS Ourang Medan, a ghost ship whose entire crew was allegedly killed under mysterious circumstances (discovered with terrified expressions on their faces), was first reported by a Dutch-Indonesian newspaper in February. Finally, on August 7, the first of over two hundred fires was set on a farm in Macomb, Illinois, by what some believed to be a poltergeist, while others claim a disturbed teenager with pyrokinetic capabilities was the culprit.

her dead nephew, Lucas! Phyllis began to make plans to move out, even though she had nowhere else to go.

In September, neighbors visited Phyllis again and made a recommendation. They had heard that the local priest, Father Leger, in a past assignment, had gained some experience in exorcism. Perhaps they could get him to eradicate the troubled spirits that were continually torturing Phyllis. She agreed this might be her only chance to stay in the house. So, the two women visited Father Leger at the church on Valley Road and told him of the story. At first, he was hesitant to get involved, but after hearing the details, he agreed to visit the house and make his assessment.

The evening Father Leger visited Phyllis Fennell, she had tea and raisin muffins as they talked at the table. The priest had doubted the stories to this time, but suddenly, as Phyllis began to relate the story of the wailing from the upper rooms, the teacup in front of the priest began to wobble and slowly move across the table toward him. He jumped up in time to avoid a scalding message. Then a low voice, somewhat difficult to understand whispered in a grating voice. "Get out of here, now!" Father Leger, now standing, ashen but determined, agreed. "Yes, my dear, we will indeed have an exorcism in this place. Until then, you may stay in the guest house behind the parsonage."

The process for having an exorcism approved by the Church is rather lengthy. It was not until the following summer, appropriately in mid-July, that an appointed eight-man committee, laden with various paraphernalia, trudged down the lane to the deserted Fennell House. The day was hot, as is often the case in July, and the sweating men, led by Father Leger, carried their jackets on their arms. The door was difficult to open, but eventually, it relented with a loud protesting crack. Before the eight men was a dusty dining room tabletop. The room was trimmed smartly in dark oak cabinets loaded with abandoned china and cutlery haphazardly strewn on the shelves.

The men were jittery. No one from the parish except Leger had ever witnessed an exorcism rite, and twilight was quickly approaching. Since the electricity had long been cut off, the candles that each man placed on the table in front of him provided the only dreary, flickering light, casting dancing shadows eerily in dark corners of the room. When the eight took their seats around the table, Father Leger read a long prayer in Latin that none of them had ever heard. Then the priest instructed the men to open the leather-bound books each had been given to begin the rite. He also told them to persist even if afraid because each of them had been empowered by the Church to do this and would be given the strength to get through it.

*The priest commented that he believed that there were a number of distracted souls trapped in this house, but it was the committee's appointed task to concentrate on the one malicious spirit which had caused so much discomfort to the owners of the house. It would be difficult, but they must necessarily ignore the pleas of the others. As he went on, he explained the prayers, written in Latin needed powerful and precise responses from them if they were to be successful. Each man mutely nodded understanding and turned intently to his readings.*

*Father Leger, reciting loudly from his book, began to chant in a monotone like one might hear in a Medieval cathedral. Soon the rest of the men started to rhythmically respond in the same way, imitating the voice of the clergyman. At first, nothing seemed changed. Perhaps it was because the men had become enamored by their ritualistic responses.*

*Looking back, the men admitted the first thing they noticed was the room itself growing cooler—much colder than was natural. A few men absent-mindedly donned their discarded jackets as they maintained their droning prayer vigil. It was then that some of them heard what he later described as a whispering that may have at first thought to have been the wind in the nearby pines. The whispering sound became more and more pronounced until intelligible words were beginning to be understood. Out! Please leave my house; the voice once grated clearly. Several men stood in their seats, pale, with fearful expressions. The priest called out to the men that they remain strong. After a short hesitation, each settled one by one back into his seat and proceeded with his assigned oral prayers.*

*Now, the room was noticeably colder, and one man looked back at the window and noticed, despite the heat of a July night, the glass was covered with a layer of ice! Then it happened. Several loud protests appeared to come from within the walls, and the cupboard doors flew open, violently emptying the contents of the shelves and drawers onto the floor at the feet of the chanters. There was another loud male voice groaning as if in pain. Then the window—the one that had iced up—suddenly burst inward.*

*The room began to warm, and now the candles that had once barely lighted the room burned with a more significant flame. The low voices were ended. Without a word, Father Leger gestured to his men, who packed up the books and extinguished their candles. The exorcism had been completed.*

*It was not, as Father Leger had indicated to the eight men who helped him with the exorcism, the end of the strange happenings at the Fennell House, but the task of returning the malicious haunting spirit to his grave had apparently been successful. For twenty-five years people reported hauntings, voices, apparitions, music, and other things. The house exchanged hands several times until the last owner, a descendant of Margaret Fennell, decided the house was unlivable. No one could sleep there at night anymore, and there were too many bad memories. In March 1991, the house was razed in hopes of ending the hauntings. Some say, the spirits are still there and have witnessed them at certain times.*

*Perhaps. You will have to be the judge.*

*The information for this story is based on interviews with people who lived in the area back then at the time of the exorcism and on sketchy church records. Most of the people have said they heard about the exorcism but did not know much about it. I was fortunate enough to meet and interview John B. who claimed to have been one of the eight men on the committee that performed the exorcism. John was reputable and of good character. I believe him. John is dead now, and out of respect for him and his family, he must remain "John B."*

## *The Vanished Village*

*Fiddler's Green was, for most people, a happy place, not far from the village, near the intersection of Valley Road, an open meadow tucked snugly in behind the church situated on the corner off Cannelton Road. It was loosely rimmed by several shelters, a rather large gazebo near the church on the southern perimeter, and a raised dais centered as much as possible used by local entertainers, fiddlers mostly, and thus the name—fiddler's green. Saturday evening throughout the summers and warm part of the fall featured festive entertainment to the delight of residents and visitors who came for many miles for a good time. More often than not, revelers spent the night in the outbuildings and attended services at the church on Sunday morning.*

*It was during one of these times during the Great War in Europe that one young man, Thomas Grant by name, had by chance driven by in his 1915 Ford and was immediately drawn toward the merrymaking he witnessed at Fiddler's Green. Tom was one of those people who made friends easily and quickly joined in with dancing, drinking, and jubilant socializing. By midnight, Tom, exhausted from several hours of strenuous activity, figured he had achieved his personal goal of dancing at least once with every pretty girl he could find there that night. As Tom leaned casually against the wooden column of one shelter, he became aware of the unmistakable softly-*

curved silhouette of a woman. Tom was amazed he had somehow never noticed this lass all evening.

How could he have missed this girl? She was a real gem! As she stood by herself in the shadows, her dark silky hair, reaching delicately to her waist, glistened in the lights strung in the nearby shelter. Tom could not bear to leave this beauty unconquered.

"Hello, my name's Tom, Tom Grant" he blurted out. When the woman turned to him, his heart melted. Even in the dim light, her blue sapphire eyes disarmed him. Her pallid freckled complexion was further brightened by a broad even-toothed smile.

"Chloe Ann. Chloe Ann Cummings. And how are you sir?" she offered melodically with a slight curtsy. Her Irish accent was rather heavy but stirred Tom even more. "I've danced with all the girls tonight but never saw you here. Have you been here long?"

"Yes, yes. Long. I've been here quite long." Chloe Ann seemed to be speaking distantly as though in deep thought. "Do you mind if I sit with you for a while? Maybe you'd care to dance?" "I'd like to talk, but if you do not mind, I'd rather not attempt to dance. Some say I have not the legs for dancing," she answered, her eyes raised pleadingly.

Tom Grant would have preferred to dance, just to get his bearings so to speak. He felt he could often assess a woman better on the dance floor and this girl was presently a big mystery to him. In any event, he was tired, and a long talk might be just what he needed.

For over an hour, Tom and Chole exchanged information with each other about where they lived, what they did, and what they liked. As it turned out, Chloe Ann indicated she lived nearby, a few miles west from here in a little town named New England. "Originally Nova Anglise," Chloe Ann revealed. "It was changed later to sound more English.

By this time there were few people left on the Green. The musicians had already packed and gone. A few men were asleep in the gazebo. "Where are your folks, Chloe Ann? It's a little late for a girl to be out," Tom said. "Oh, I came myself, Tom. As I do many Saturday evenings. The way is not long," she said with a lilting voice. It seemed to Tom she was hinting that she needed a ride. Tom could not expect anything better! After the time spent together, Tom found Chloe Ann to be the most interesting and alluring woman he had ever met, and he had hoped to develop a relationship with her.

"My car, I think you would like it, Chloe Ann. It's a new V-8! I could have you home in a whiz!" Chloe Ann smiled and nodded slightly. "I would like that Tom Grant. You and your V-8."

*Tom took Chloe Ann gently by the arm to his car, where she glided silently across the leather seats. When Tom got in, she laid her head on his shoulder as Tom backed out and turned right on the main road. Tom would typically want to show off the power of his new car, but for once he wanted to enjoy every minute of this experience. The ride usually was little more than ten minutes away, but that night the trip took more than a quarter of an hour.*

*Finally, Chloe Ann directed Tom to turn right, and they followed a winding road that ended among a scattering of small cottages that Tom thought looked like pictures he had seen in brochures of picturesque houses in Ireland. Very quaint. Somehow the cabins reminded him very much of Chloe Ann. Then he went around the car, opened the door for the girl, and they walked together up a flagstone walkway to one of the cottages.*

*"Can I see you again, Chloe?" Tom whispered anxiously. "I guess that's up to you Tom Grant," she said coyly. "I'm not planning on going anywhere. I'll be somewhere around here if you want to find me." "I'll be back tomorrow then," Tom nervously replied as he looked away, not wanting to reveal his true feelings so quickly. In reality, Tom desperately wanted to kiss Chloe Ann, but by the time he turned back, Chloe Ann was gone.*

*Tom was ecstatic over his new love. That night, instead of driving home, he slept in his car near the creek, awoke the next morning, bathed in the creek, went into Cannelton Inn and had a breakfast of ham, eggs, and fried potatoes. Refreshed and determined, Tom set out for the village of New England. The night before had been dark, but Tom was sure he remembered every inch of the way. But when he turned up the lane off the main road, he did not remember how washed out the road had been, and it worsened as his car climbed the winding road to the town. Suddenly he was in the open—no village, nothing! He was sure he had made the right turn. Tom got out of his car and looked around. He immediately recognized the excavations associated with coal stripping.*

*This place is nothing but a strip mine! Where did I make the wrong turn? For several hours Tom traced and retraced his route, but he could not locate the town. As a last resort, he knew he would have to ask someone for directions. On his way back, as he passed the church, he noticed a few people on the grounds at Fiddler's Green. With a spray of gravel, Tom spun his car into the parking area and braked near an old man raking shredded paper into a basket.*

*"Say there, my man, could you help me? Could you tell me how to get to New England?" The man looked up sadly but did not answer and went on*

with his work. Tom was bothered that the man was ignoring him. "This is quite important," Tom persisted to the man. "You see, I've met someone there, and I've got to see her again. I-I think I'm in love. You've got to help me."

The old man leaned his rake against an oak tree and turned solemnly. "Sir, you are not the first to be won over by this particular young lady's charms. She is well-known around Fiddler's Green. Now and then she meets someone here, and they take her home—to New England."

"Yes, yes, that's the one. So where is New England?" "It's right where you thought it was. There on the top of the hill." "But there's nothing there but strip mines," argued Tom. "That's right, sir. And once, thirty years ago, there was a New England right there, but now it's gone. Purchased and covered over."

"But what about the girl I met…" Tom started. "Chloe Ann Cummings…" began the man. "Yes, yes. Chloe Ann Cummings" repeated Tom, now shaking. "How did you know her name?" "I know this will be a shock to you, friend, but the young lady's been dead now for over twenty years—killed in a horrible accident by a freight wagon carrying brick along the road as Chloe Ann walked this way. Both of her legs were cut off in the accident. She was on the way to Fiddler's Green you know. She's hitched a ride home so many times now, and every time the gentleman has come by looking for her."

Tom Grant was stunned, speechless, felt faint and weak. A few minutes later he was on his knees in the dust of Fiddler's Green and was violently sick to his stomach.

This story was related to me in 1981 by Mr. Jared Blue, previously of Valley Road, then in his 90's and now deceased. He swore the story was true and once claimed to have one night taken Chloe Ann home to New England himself.

## Analysis of Evidence: Source Derivation

While the creators of the dubious Sprucevale legends of Jake's Lock, the Little Boy and the Mushroom Lady provided little to no researchable particulars such as exact dates or even full names in most cases, Oswald provides enough detail in his tales of Cannelton to conduct analysis. For instance, the Fennell family was one of the last owners of the allegedly haunted brick home, which sat vacant for many years on Cannelton Road.

*Right*: Steps leading up from Cannelton Road are all that remains of St. Rose Church.

*Below*: St. Rose Bulletin, including Teresa Fennell, 1955. *Author's family history archives.*

As a child, I once explored the abandoned house with my cousins, daring one another to look into the basement for the bloodstained wall. The version of the story I knew growing up was far less detailed, attributing the ghastly murder of the baby to its incessant crying driving the baby's mother insane. I knew it as the "Fennell House" even though ownership changed hands a few times after Ms. Fennell passed away. It was vacant as far back as I can remember. My parents considered purchasing the property shortly before it was torn down. However, it was structurally unsound.

The church mentioned in both stories also existed, and Father Leger pastored there from 1932 until sometime before his death in 1955.[96] Much of my family attended this church. After a new facility was built two miles away on State Route 51 in 1964, the diocese had the first St. Rose of Lima structure torn down.

I can find no other reference to an exorcism performed in Cannelton, and the diocese isn't apt to discuss such activities. My grandparents bought their home, which was a short walk away, in 1956, becoming neighbors of Teresa Fennell, who was also a member of the congregation. They do not recall learning of an exorcism in the tight-knit community.

## *The Fennell House*

Just as accurate provable details help to promote confidence in the authenticity of stories, simple errors introduce doubt. The Irish Catholic Fennell clan did include a Margaret who passed away in 1953, but none of the immediate family was named Phyllis. The family did include a Catherine P. Fennell, but I was unable to determine if her middle name was Phyllis. She died of leukemia in a Beaver Falls hospital in 1960. Teresa Fennell, a schoolteacher all her life, was the last Fennell to own the property. She passed away in 1978. As established earlier, the house was built by George Foulks in 1820, not by B. Clayton during the Civil War. Finally, photos provided by the Little Beaver Historical Society dated 2001, just prior to the Fennell House being torn down, verify that it was not demolished in 1991 as claimed in the story. Many former Cannelton residents have heard tales of the Fennell House being haunted. Several shared them on the Pig Lady Facebook site, but significant details provided in John B's version of the Fennell House story are too easily disproven. Perhaps John B confused or conflated the Fennell House with another home built by B. Clayton.

The Fennell House, as it appeared in 2001. *Courtesy of the Little Beaver Historical Society.*

## *The Vanishing Village*

The first irregularity I noticed on my initial read-through of this fascinating tale was that Ford did not produce a car powered by a V-8 in 1915. The Model T had an inline four-cylinder. Ford's "Flathead" V-8, Pretty Boy Floyd's engine of choice, didn't appear until 1932. Second, I thought it odd that as a local born and raised I'd never heard of Fiddler's Green, a village named New England or Chloe Ann Cummings. A small community did exist on the hillside in the State Game Lands #285. Locals know it today as Stanley's Knob or Mount Nebo. I've explored the ruins myself. The old abandoned road trace is still visible across from the intersection of Watt's Mill and Cannelton Roads. Families living here in the late 1800s likely worked in the coal mines or the nearby Little Beaver Woolen Mill.

While I thoroughly enjoy all of Oswald's peculiar tales, I admittedly spent little effort in examining this story for two reasons. First, my ignorance of Chloe is unusual considering my familiarity with Cannelton. None of my relatives know the story either, and I could find no additional references to Chloe outside of Oswald's story. Second, and most important, I immediately

Vanished Village ruins.

recognized the tell-tale signs of the vanishing hitchhiker urban myth even before entirely reading the essay. Nearly as widespread as the Lady in White, versions of the vanishing hitchhiker story can be found across the country as well as in several European nations, one of the most famous being Resurrection Mary in Chicago. The fable is so widespread that Disney satirizes hitchhiking ghosts in its Haunted Mansion attractions.

According to *Lore of the Ghost*, two American anthropologists studied the hitchhiking ghost legend in 1952, finding seventy-nine different versions across the United States, which could generally be divided into four standard themes.[97] Of the seventy-nine stories, eleven fall into the third theme category: "A young man meets a girl at a place of entertainment, often a dance and offers to drive her home. On the way, the girl complains of being cold, and the motorist offers his coat or jacket, and then she asks to be dropped off at a cemetery and disappears. The motorist later discovers that the girl he met was in fact dead."[98]

# 6
# KNOBS, FRAUDS AND THE CANNELTON SUN GOD

## WELCOME TO THE ROCK

Family traditions often involve commonplace rituals intended to maintain a dynastic structure. Regular Sunday dinners at a patriarch's home are a useful mechanism for passing familial history and traditions down to new generations. It's one of the customary methods with which culture is preserved in middle America. My family does this, but we also hike to a boulder carved like a human head every autumn, daring one another to eat the most disgusting prepackaged food possible. Why? Because it's weird, and in our clan the Cannelton Sun God demands sacrifices.

Growing up, the site Ira Mansfield refers to as Painter's Knob was known as Indian Rock to my family and friends. After summer days swimming at the Hippie Bridge, we would hike up its steep slopes to look for arrowheads or to see who could throw rocks farthest off an eroding portion caused by long ago strip mining. No one in the neighborhood knew definitively why the strange boulder was on top or what it meant to whoever sculpted it. Ask three different Canneltonites, and you'll likely receive three different answers. A Native American sacrificial altar, an ancient grain pestle, the work of an artist for a long-lost love or even an oddly placed birdbath are all standard explanations for the strange petroglyph.*

---

* A petroglyph is a carving or drawing usually on a rock made by ancient people.

*Above*: Boulder at Painter's Knob. *From Mansfield,* Historical Collections: Little Beaver River Valleys.

*Left*: The Indian Rock or Cannelton Sun-god.

In Cannelton, after the Pig Lady, Indian Rock is probably the strangest bit of local folklore. Like Barbara, the earliest known written reference to Indian Rock is made by the same man, Ira Mansfield. Is this coincidence? Perhaps there is nothing peculiar to discover, as Mansfield is likely the first local folklorist with the means to publish these tales. Or could the happenstance of these two famous legends be the work of a privileged, quixotic and restless mind? Based on the evidence I've uncovered, an argument can be made for either case.

# Knobs

Being a Civil War infantryman, it's safe to assume Mansfield developed a unique appreciation for high ground. This may be why he refers to Painter's Knob and others in Cannelton and the local area on fourteen separate occasions in his two most well-known books. During the Chattanooga campaign, he participated in the bloody battle of Lookout Mountain, in which his unit was likely one of several utilized in General Thomas's bold assault on Orchard Knob.[99] This skirmish led to the eventual lifting of the Confederate siege of Union forces at Chattanooga. Later, during the Atlanta campaign, he played a part in the battle to take Bald Knob while fighting with the Army of the Ohio.[100] War leaves an indelible effect on those unfortunate enough to have experienced it. I believe this to be the reason why Mansfield chose to call two of the high points in the Little Beaver Creek Valley Orchard and Bald Knob as a tribute.

Bald Knob, now called Round Knob, is in Middleton Township, Columbiana County, south of the middle fork of Little Beaver Creek. At 1,436 feet, it's the fourth-highest peak in Ohio. Mansfield corrected himself in later essays, referring to Round Knob by its proper name. However, in one curious stanza, he claimed, "Bald Knob, 1437 feet above sea level, has a noted school house, requiring children to brave the weird tales and is locally known as the Witch Hollow School, whose every teacher has proved a witch."[101] This was most likely a tongue-in-cheek reference for the benefit of the second Robin Hood Club members—the majority of whom were teachers.* The Witch Hollow School did exist, having several mentions in *East Liverpool Evening Review* archives.

---

* The first Robin Hood Club was a men's organization that lasted from 1865 to 1908. The second Robin Hood Club for women began in 1903 and ended sometime after Ira Mansfield—the club's benefactor—died in 1919.

Orchard Knob is somewhere near Watt's Mill Road in Cannelton. Mansfield wrote, "The Mill-dam furnishes extended pools of water for boating, fishing, bathing and nature studies, while nearby is Orchard Knob, giving extended views into Pennsylvania, Ohio, and Virginia."[102] The only orchard in the area at the time was on his property above the mines, indicating it is near his former home on Ridge Road.

## BOUQUET KNOB

Mansfield and his Civil War veteran comrades of the first Robin Hood Club named another knob in honor of a much earlier military event. Bouquet is a hill behind the United Methodist Church in Negley, Ohio. After breaking the Siege of Fort Pitt during Pontiac's Rebellion, British colonel Henry Bouquet assembled a small army consisting of militia from Pennsylvania and Virginia, as well as regular (professional military) Scottish Highlanders. He used this force to invade tribal lands in the Northwest Territory (in what is now Ohio) with a goal of retrieving colonial prisoners. In describing Bouquet's epic incursion, a member of the Robin Hood Club wrote:

> *Sunday, October 7th. Passing a high ridge, they had a fine prospect of an extensive country on the right which in general appeared level with an abundance of tall timber. The camp No. 6 lies at the foot of a steep ascent in a rich valley on a strong ground; three sides thereof surrounded by a hollow and on the fourth side a small hill which was occupied by a detached guard. This day's march was six miles, sixty-five perches. Camp No. 6 on the hemlock bluff, across Little Beaver from lands now owned by I.F. Mansfield, and the small hill is now known as Bouquet Knob.*[103]

Ira Mansfield and his first Robin Hood Club members also believed Bouquet's forces stayed in Negley on what is now known as the LeBate Farm property upon the army's return in 1764. Built in 1857, the house and barn Mansfield once owned are still standing as of this writing but have been vacant for years and are suffering from neglect. In another more detailed essay about Bouquet's incursion into Indian lands from Fort Pitt, Mansfield wrote,

> *In 1750 a Virginian named Smith was taken prisoner and held in their camp at the old Beaver dam near (East) Palestine, and later taken to*

Bouquet Farm barn, present day.

*another larger camp near Tamarack swamp east of Columbiana. Here he was compelled to run the gauntlet of boys and squaws before adoption. They also killed and scalped a settler on Long's run and sent his wife and children to their village. Without delay Col. Bouquet rapidly pursued the fleeing Indians by the Tuscarora trail, camping overnight on the bluff overlooking the present site of Negley, O., and the isolated knob nearby was occupied as his outpost by the Scotch Highlanders. This knob under Bouquet's name stands as a monument to mark the memory of one of the bravest and most successful heroes who ever trod American soil. On his return with 300 white prisoners rescued from the Indians, Bouquet, and his army, owing to the high water in Little Beaver, they encamped for two days on the farm now owned by Captain I. F. Mansfield, near the Bouquet Knob. From this camp, one woman escaped from the Scotch guards and returned to her Indian husband.*[104]

Mansfield bought Bouquet Knob and used it for one of his many Robin Hood Club campsites. The alley leading up the hill today is still named Bouquet. A passage in the 1905 *History of Columbiana County* either corroborates, may have been the origins of or, more likely, was influenced by Mansfield's Negley-centered Bouquet Expedition encampment theories:

> *There is a slight conflict of dates, but a consensus of several authorities at hand would seem to show that it was on Monday, October 8th that Colonel Bouquet and his army encamped at in one record is given as camp No. 7 in Columbiana County, at the beautiful spot near Negley, which has since been known as Camp Bouquet. One authority says: "Camp No. 7 lies at the foot of a beautiful knoll, commanding the ground around it, and is distant eleven miles, one-quarter and forty-nine perches from the last encampment."*
>
> *Keeping on their course, they came two days after to a point where the Indian path they had been following so long divided—the two branches leading off at a wide angle. The trees at the forks were covered with hieroglyphics, describing the various battles the Indians had fought and told the number of scalps they had taken, etc. This point was at the southern point of the present county of Columbiana.*[105]

The discovery of an original map drawn by Thomas Hutchins, a participant of the Bouquet expedition, exposed a different possible camp location according to *The Orderly Book of Colonel Henry Bouquet's Expedition against the Ohio Indians*, written by E.G. Williams:

> *The 38-mile camp was designated No. 6 in the journal. The location of the site has been a matter of conjecture for many years. Various writers have placed it where it seemed convenient to them, and local tradition has confused it with the site of an annual encampment of veterans of the Civil War held there for many years and called Camp Bouquet in honor of the first great leader of civilization in Columbiana County. Since then, however, the very map drawn by the hand of Thomas Hutchins himself has come to light, no further doubt can exist as to the precise spot. It is the original draft, plotted each evening as the expedition progressed, from the field survey notes of the day. It represents the sector 1-3/4 miles before the crossing of the Big Beaver to approximately 3-5/8 miles west of the Pennsylvania-Ohio line. It ends at a point in the creek bottom just below the Mount Zion Church in Middleton Township, Columbiana County, Ohio.*[106]

This work, transcribed in 1960, names and describes every expedition camp by number. Clearly, the author was referring to Ira's first Robin Hood Club when he stated: "local tradition has confused it with the site of an

The second Robin Hood Club at Camp Bouquet. *From Mansfield,* Ohio and Pennsylvania Reminiscences.

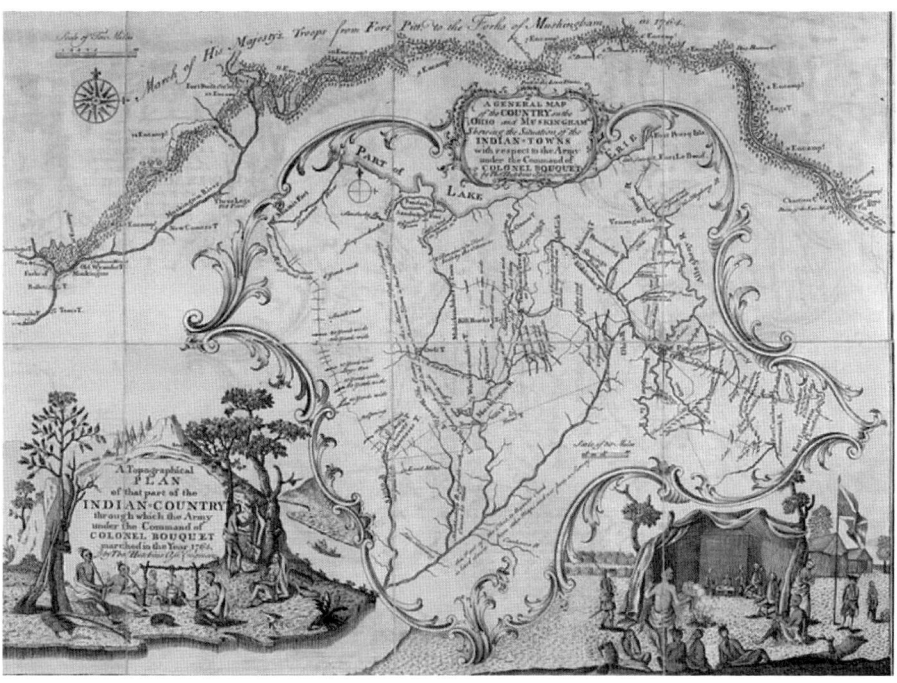

Thomas Hutchins's Bouquet Expedition map. *From Williams,* The Orderly Book of Colonel Henry Bouquet's Expedition against the Ohio Indians, 1764.

annual encampment of veterans of the Civil War held there for many years and called Camp Bouquet." Both Mansfield and Williams name this location as Camp 6, whereas the 1905 *History of Columbiana County* claims Camp 7 is the site of Camp Bouquet. Coincidentally, Camp 7 as identified by Williams is very near Sprucevale. I'm somewhat surprised this history hasn't resulted in yet another fable for that locale.

Had I been a Robin Hood Club member, I'd have argued vehemently that Colonel Bouquet did not deserve a single accolade. Yes, his rescue of captured frontiersmen is commendable, but this man is also responsible for the intentional spread of smallpox to natives, the majority of whom were noncombatants, by gifts of infected blankets from Fort Pitt. This heinous act of biological warfare is still widely known today, but its attribution to Bouquet has faded. Some estimates suggest up to three-quarters of the Native American population in the Northwest Territories died from smallpox outbreaks afterward.

Approximate location of Camp 7 in 2018, according to Williams.

LEGENDS & LORE OF LITTLE BEAVER CREEK

# NATIVE FORTS ALONG THE LITTLE BEAVER?

While Colonel Bouquet's mark on the area is proven, an often-mentioned detail in Mansfield's books caught me completely unaware. He references possible archaeological native remnants of ancient fortifications at Bouquet and Round Knob on three separate occasions in his books. While prehistoric mound-building cultures indeed existed in the Ohio River Valley, I was unaware of ancient ruins in Middleton Township.

> *The earliest evidence of man's existence on the Beaver rivers is shown in the graves of Indians among the granite boulders and the peculiar lines of fortifications at Bouquet's Knob, Frederick, and Milford. The literature on the subject is extensive and stands as a monument of our ignorance, but the findings of skulls are not conclusive evidence of man's existence here before the Ice Age. What adds interest and is evidence of man's existence previous to the Indians is that in these granite boulder graves, we find clay idols, shells, beads and copper spears, buried below the markings made by the Ice Age. All these implements only confuse the theory that men floated here from Asia, as the cultures of the prehistorical people, bears no traces of foreign nations. Our early inhabitants disclose some carvings, mounds and fortifications, but they failed to grasp the idea of communication, using metals in cold state, transporting everything on their backs, and spent their time in petty warfare and in the grossest superstitions. There is a fascination in studying him even as a savage, and in investigating his remains, which attests his occupancy of all our territory.*[107]

> *Nearby is Round Knob 1400 feet elevation carrying a mound builders stone fort.*[108]

> *From this camp excursions made to Round Knob 1437 feet above sea level—this being the second highest point in Ohio. On the top are remains of a stone fort from the Mound Builders age.*[109]

Is it possible ancient native ruins are located in the Little Beaver watershed? Noted Ohio historian James L. Murphy was skeptical, describing Mansfield's writings on the subject as "elusive and romantic"—however, one doesn't have to travel far to find a parallel:

*In 1749, The Ohio Company of Virginia planned to establish a storehouse at Red Stone Old Fort. This site derived its name from an ancient mound builder earthwork in the immediate area that resembled an old fortification. These earthworks were circular in nature and were located on a hill that overlooks present Brownsville PA.*[110]

I contacted Dr. Jarrod Burks and inquired about the legitimacy of Ira Mansfield's claims. Dr. Burks is the director of geophysical surveys at Ohio Valley Archaeology and is passionate about surveying and preserving Ohio's ancient earthworks. He is unaware of the Middleton Township sites mentioned by Mansfield, but he did reveal that two circular enclosures are located in nearby Jefferson County. He also pointed me toward the 1914 Archeological Atlas of Ohio, which discloses locations of petroglyphs, burial sites and mounds in Columbiana County, one of which appears to be labeled on or very near Bouquet Knob.[111]

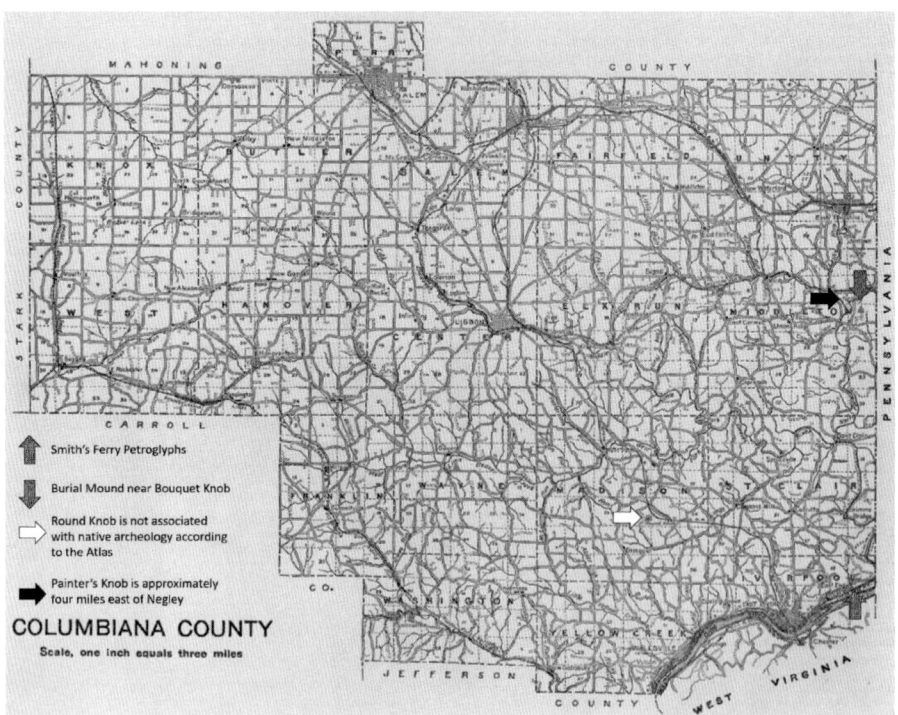

*Archaeological Atlas of Ohio*: Locations of known Native American Archaeological sites mentioned by Mansfield are shaded gray. Arrows added by the author.

Ira was well read and involved in the preservation of Ohio and Pennsylvania history. He was almost certainly aware of the early archaeological research into the mound-building culture, especially Fort Ancient earthworks of Warren County, Ohio, which were purchased and made into Ohio's first state park during his heyday in 1891.

## Grave Consequence

Unfortunately, amateur archaeology was a lucrative fad in Mansfield's time. Like the prehistoric fossils Mansfield sold for personal gain, native relics were widely collected for profit without regard for cultural preservation.[112] A passage in one of his books seems to reveal that the Little Beaver River Valley was once replete with petroglyphs, ostensibly lending credibility to the possible Native American origin of Indian Rock. His past-tense description suggests most were removed for undisclosed reasons:

> *In many places in our counties on rocks are picture carvings dating back to the Indians. They represent men, animals, birds, and fish. Above Milford, on the West-fork, are several; on Leslie's run were two groups; on Long's run and near Cannelton were several, but at the mouth of the Little Beaver on the bedrocks of the Ohio river we find the greatest variety, including figures of Indians with arms, birds, animals, and their tracks. On the corner-stones of the old mound Builder's' fort on Bald [Round] Knob were several animals pictured. These early carvings prove that man was here at a very early period, dating back to the Glacial period.*[113]

The hieroglyphics near the mouth of the Little Beaver are well documented and are curiously called Indian Rocks. They were considered to be one of the best collections created by the ancient Monongahela people sometime between AD 1200–1750, before being covered over by the Ohio River when a dam was erected in East Liverpool in the early 1900s.[114] They were last visible during a drought in 1960.

Sadly, the looting wasn't restricted to native carvings. While it might seem shocking now, native burial site desecration was common practice until it became outlawed by the Native American Graves Preservation and Repatriation Act in 1990. Robbing a Massachusett tribal grave was one of the first activities of the Mayflower pilgrims.[115] Thomas Jefferson excavated a burial mound on his property in 1764 (the same year of Bouquet's expedition into Ohio), and the U.S. Army issued orders to collect Indian skeletal specimens for the Army Medical Museum in 1865, the year Ira was discharged from service. Realizing this, it is unsurprising that in separately written essays about relics and land contracts, Mansfield freely admits to pilfering graves located on knobs at both his Negley and Cannelton properties:

ALSO, IN 1764
*The Beast of Gévaudan, an oversized gray wolf or, according to some, a werewolf, began a three-year killing spree in south-central France.*

> *It is a natural desire that we should love to travel over the past and learn what we can from the silent years of the sweet by and by. We cannot resurrect those who lived in the past, but we can gather items of interest from various sources. As to the antiquity of man, careful research along the Little Beaver has revealed nothing beyond the Indians and Mound Builders. Many relics from graves and early settlers made from copper, flints, and shells recovered, being on display in the Mansfield collections. At Bouquet's Knob, near Negley was a stone ring fort and on opening a grave revealed a mother with a child buried in a sitting position on a bench shelf, decorated with a string of bone beads, holding a clay dish and copper spear knife. On the Middle and West Forks, are three old stone line forts, from which have been secured burnt clay dishes, white and red flints.*[116]

> *The above agreement was for fifteen acres, being the north-east angle of Cannel tract. No deed was given or record made of the agreement which provides that fence as now established, making a straight line on the eastern boundary, shall be the line. The pioneer settlers had made his angle to include a cabin settlement with clearing made by William Sproat, followed by claiming entire Cannel tract. Re-surveys showed errors of their claim and gave back to Cannel tract this cabin clearing, which was an old Indian camping place. Close by this camp, on the spring run ravine, still stands an ancient oak, fully 300 years old, with large burl or knot on one side. This tree marks an old Indian cache in which was found pots for melting and pouring lead, and many stone and flint implements. All these have been carefully mounted, and along with other local collections are on display at the homestead. Visitors are always welcome. Several of the Indian graves at the Cannel Knob were opened—one grave the Indian was placed in a sitting position, having a number of implements and more than one hundred flint arrow points, in a circle around him.*[117]

Painter's Knob.

Mansfield proudly mounted and displayed his relics in sixteen cases at his Cannelton home, "where you can go around the world without wasting time or money." He lists among the collection Indian spear and arrow flints, Indian pipes, tom-tom emblems and war clubs, Indian war bonnets, bead garters and bead coats, mound builder's flints, mound axes, Indian pestles, skinning stones and stone emblems.[118] I assume not all were collected on his properties, but according to Ira's own words, some of these items were the plunder of Little Beaver watershed grave robbery.*

Growing up, I often heard stories of Indian Rock being haunted, but unlike most ghost stories, these alleged disturbances lack a definitive cause. Once while camping at the site during my teenage years, a friend said he was awoken by a sound outside his tent. His investigation led to the discovery of a distraught-looking warrior whose shape dissipated shortly after being observed. To this day, I remain skeptical of my friend's motivations for sharing the story the next morning. Indian burial site desecration was a familiar source of paranormal activity in horror movies back then. We were big fans of films like *The Shining, Pet Sematary* and *The Amityville Horror*. I assumed this theme and Indian Rock's mythos influenced my friend's suggestive imagination back then, but now I can't help wonder if the distasteful activities of our forefathers spawned the phenomenon.

## FRAUDS AND THE SUN GOD

Since the mid-1970s, Painter's Knob (Indian Rock) has been a site of controversy within academic circles. In 1975, the Department of the Interior surveyed the Little Beaver Creek and acknowledged the carved boulder at its peak to have native origins. Before this, there was little interest in the site from professional anthropologists, archaeologists or historians alike, but the published site survey caused a stir. The report noted that "the Painter's Knob boulder is a large granite boulder with prehistoric carvings resembling a human head with eyes, nose, and mouth depressed in the rock. These features were probably used as mortars to grind grain."[119]

Skeptics ever since have clamored to debunk this claim. In a 1978 article in the journal *Pennsylvania Archaeologist*, James L. Murphy argues that the possibility of Indian Rock's native origin is suspect because the lack of wear

---

* Case no. 9—Pressed Orchids, can be seen in Darlington's Second Greersburg Academy museum (a building Ira constructed). Others were in the possession of the Beaver Area Heritage Foundation, which as recently as 2014 displayed parts of them in a Native American relics exhibit. In *Ohio and Pennsylvania Reminiscences*, Mansfield wrote that he donated the rest to the Youngstown Historic Society and Beaver College (now Arcadia University).

on a square mortar is suspicious. He then criticizes Mansfield's motivations for photographing the monument in 1916:

> More telling, perhaps, is the fact that there are no known accounts of this odd carving prior to 1916 when it was illustrated, without comment, in Ira F. Mansfield's Reminiscences. Mansfield, while preserving much interesting and valuable information in his several books, must be considered of doubtful authority, for he was intent on filling the valley of Little Beaver Creek with as much legend and local color as possible, peopling it with ghosts and mound builders, to amuse and delight his merry band of "schoolmarms," as he termed them.[120]

Murphy also offers as evidence an interview he conducted in 1959, with the then seventy-five-year-old Charles "Possum" May, a lifelong Cannelton resident. May recalled hearing as a boy that the "Sun God" was carved by "an eccentric itinerant." May claims to have seen the man, who he was told carved the stone, and that he had known people who could recall a time when the rock had not been etched. May could not remember the carver's name.

Murphy submitted one last piece of evidence for doubting Indian Rock's authenticity. He cites a colleague, James Swauger, from the Carnegie Museum of Natural History who visited the site in 1974 and "has indicated to me that he too, considers the 'mortar' to be non-aboriginal." He concludes that the carving is the work of an unknown itinerant circa 1880.[121] Later, in 1990, James Swauger also published a piece on the topic in *Pennsylvania Archaeologist*, in which he recounts Murphy's evidence but largely offers up nothing new except:

> "Possum" May was correct according to George Swetnam and Helene Smith's A Guidebook to Historic Western Pennsylvania (1976:32): "Stone Face was created by Charles Jones, an eccentric who carved the face in a huge rock, with two round hollows for eyes, one for a mouth, and a square depression for a nose, so that water would collect for birds to drink." At the moment, nothing more is known about Charles Jones than that contained in the Swetnam-Smith citation, but coupled with Murphy's "Possum" May statement, it is reasonable to assume that it was Charles Jones who carved the "Sun God" petroglyph.[122]

An article in a 1998 edition of the *Beaver County Times* citing an earlier 1980 *Valley Tribune* article offered another eccentric as the boulder's creator. The piece reports that Margaret Ross, a Beaver County educator and historian, believed the stone was carved by a man named Charles Morgan. Morgan was a great hunter, but his mind was weak. He felt the spot needed a birdbath because birds could not find water on the knob even though the creek is not far away. The *Times* article then insinuates Murphy's eccentric itinerant and Ross's weak-minded hunter are one and the same and that members of the White family, who once owned the property, assert the boulder was carved before 1875.[123]

Could Charles Morgan and Charles Jones be the same person? Might Ira Mansfield have known the true origins of the carving but instead of cruelly chronicling the oddities of an infirm man chose to add flavor to local native lore as an alternative? It's very possible, but without dedicated anthropologic research, we may never know.

While I'm not qualified to argue anthropologic analysis, I am surprised by the poor research method (those in my profession call it tradecraft) utilized to discredit the boulder's potential Native American pedigree. At least in the latter two instances, circular reporting appears pervasive, while the credibility of the original source material is not established. First Murphy claims Mansfield illustrated the boulder without comment in his 1916 book *Ohio and Pennsylvania Reminiscences*. It is true that Mansfield's 1916 work included the photo at the head of a story without statement beyond its caption, but another essay in the book contains this passage: "One boulder in Darlington township, having the features of a man's face, is still known as the Sun-God, marking an Indian burying ground."[124]

Murphy's credibility as a researcher takes a minor hit here in my opinion, and it's not improved by citing groupthink proclivities* as argumentation to bolster the legitimacy of his analysis (i.e., my friend at the Carnegie Museum thinks so too). Other than this, the only evidence provided is an interview with an elderly man who couldn't remember the carver's name and Murphy's opinion that the carving doesn't look aboriginal without explanation. These points could be significant if they were better developed, but the reader is left to make a judgment without further clarification as to why these points should be meaningful.

Swauger, who is an expert in the field of native petroglyphs, presents even less evidence yet claims to have further solidified the analysis by rehashing Murphy's contributions to the assessment seemingly without researching the

---

* Groupthink occurs when likeminded individuals value harmony and coherence over accurate analysis and critical evaluation.

evidence himself* and by citing a travel guide. Curiously, one of the authors of the book referenced by Swauger is the famed folklorist George Swetnam,† who included Ira Mansfield's version of Barbara Davidson's story in his anthology *Devils, Ghosts, and Witches: Occult Folklore of the Upper Ohio Valley*. The other author, Helene Smith, now believes the Indian Rock engraver was Johnny Appleseed.

## *Sun God Rock and Johnny Appleseed*

*Today a lone glacial rock still serves birds near Cannelton, PA. While working on the* Guidebook to Historic Western Pennsylvania *(University of Pittsburgh Press) I crawled over a rickety bridge to reach a unique 5 X 4 rock on top of a high hill—Painter's Knob—to photograph it for the book.*

*At the foot of the hill is Little Beaver Creek. According to legend, an eccentric itinerant carved the rock and also laid a line of boulders across the stream. This huge bird bath and feeder was designed to resemble a human head with round holes for eyes and a square mouth for holding water.*

*Dear Ones,*

*Not until yesterday when I was eating a tart apple did it occur to me decades after the book was published that Johhny Appleseed (John Chapman) probably made this tribute to the birds. He was a vegetarian, loved animals and was disturbed when anyone treated them cruelly.*

*As a member of the Swedenborgian Church, he preached along the way as he slept in the woods and built fires for warmth and cooking. He avoided interrupting the lives of his fellow creatures he saw along the way.*

*Both he and the unknown eccentric itinerant were interested in agriculture and nurseries. Chapman wore a tin pan for a hat, makeshift clothing and walked in his bare feet as he spread apple seeds on his journey.*

*Chapman never married and spent his life planting seeds in Ohio, Pennsylvania, Illinois, Indiana and West Virginia. He died in 1845. The stone was carved in the 1800s. I really think the mysterious stone mason was Johnny Appleseed.*[125]

---

* Swauger parroted Murphy's claim that Mansfield provided nothing but a photo of the boulder without comment.
† George was the editor of and contributor to *Keystone Folklore Quarterly*.

I've come to realize that without new scientific data, it is probably impossible to endorse one Indian Rock origin theory over the others. Utilizing many analytic reasoning techniques failed to validate the previously referenced suppositions. I exhausted the tried-and-true methods. Analysis of competing hypotheses, deductive reasoning, linchpin analysis—all ended in a perplexing stalemate. Then an idea arose—devil's advocacy.*

Could Indian Rock be a simple, but accurate title? We already know the area is replete with a true, but little understood, native history. The European narrative is but a speck of the human existence in the Cannelton timeline considering anthropologic evidence in the area dates back eight-thousand-plus years. Without solid contrary information, why not?

Study the maps and logs of early European explorers, and you'll find that some antique lines of communication are still used today. British General Braddock used a well-known Indian path called Nemacolin's to build his famous road to the savage lands of Western Pennsylvania. Parts of another renowned trail called Tuscarora or Tuscarawas also act as a road in Beaver County today. The 1891 edition of *The History of the Upper Ohio Valley* describes this path:

> *But of the four trails leading out of Fort Duquesne, the most important, as well as the most interesting to people of this county, was the one known as the "Tuscarora Path," starting at Logstown [near Beaver] and crossing the Pennsylvania line into Columbiana County on the east line of Middleton Township and winding from there in a southwesterly direction through the townships of Elk Run, Center, Wayne and Franklin. Whenever the savages made a foray on the unprotected frontiers of Pennsylvania and Virginia, they traversed in gloomy silence this trail, and when returning with the fruits of their horrible atrocities, the bleeding scalps of their victims and helpless women and children doomed to a captivity worse than death, the "Tuscarora Path" was the line of their hideous triumphal march.*[126]

The Tuscarora people were one of the six nations forming the Iroquois Confederacy, which ruled these lands at the time of European conquest. The Tuscarora believed in the supernatural, and they claimed their ancestors were plagued by many monsters. One, in particular, arises from mass graves or is created from a violent murder scene in which the severed head of a victim grows to enormous size to seek revenge. This demon's name was

---

* Devil's advocacy is a structured analytic technique used to challenge a single strongly held view or a group consensus by promoting a convincing alternative.

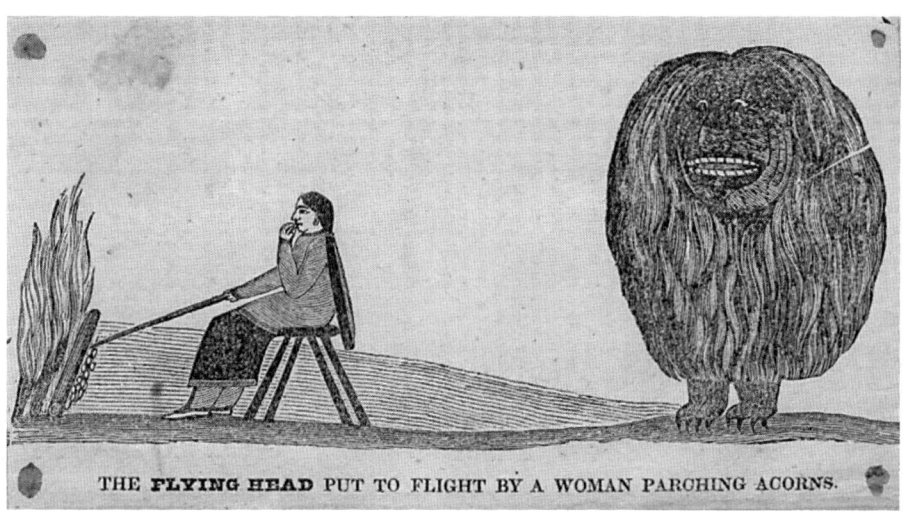

Konearaunehneh (Flying Head Monster). *From Cusick,* Sketches of Ancient History of the Six Nations.

insipidly translated into English as the Flying Head. In describing the beast, Elias Johnson, a Tuscarora chief, explained the phenomenon in 1891.

> *The first enemy that appeared to question their power or disturb their peace was the fearful phenomenon of Ko-nea-rah-yah-neh or the flying heads. The heads were enveloped in beard and hair, flaming like fire; they were of monstrous size and shot through the air with the speed of meteors. Human power was not adequate to cope with them. The priests pronounced them a flowing power of some mysterious influence, and it remained with the priests alone to expel them by their magic power.*
>
> *Drum and rattle and enchantments were deemed more effective than arrows or clubs. One evening, after they had been plagued a long time with fearful visitations, the flying head came to the door of a lodge occupied by a single female and her dog. She was sitting composedly before the fire roasting acorns, which, as they became cooked, she deliberately took from the fire and ate. Amazement seized the flying head, who put out two huge black paws from under his streaming beard. Supposing the woman to be eating live coals he withdrew, and from that time he came no more among them.*[127]

Other Iroquois Confederacy tribes such as the Seneca and Cayuga adopted Tuscarora sagas and continued to maintain the traditions after moving into the Ohio Territory in the mid-1700s. Ohio Iroquois, or Mingos,

View from Painter's Knob.

Leslie's Run grain pestle in Negley, Ohio.

established villages along the Tuscarawas River, to which the trail led.* Tanacharison, the Mingo half-king who kept a hunting cabin along Little Beaver Creek very near Painter's Knob and convinced George Washington to start a global war, was adopted into the Seneca tribe as a child after his father's death. Might he or other Mingo in the area have carved the giant head into the glacial erratic?

If the Sun God was carved around 1880 as suggested by Murphy, then Mansfield almost certainly chose to falsify its origins. If so, his motivation for creating this myth is not apparent, as he'd already collected authentic native artifacts and displayed them, some of which are still used as museum pieces today. Ira Mansfield moved to Cannelton in 1865 and was well acquainted with the family named White who owned Painter's Knob at the time.

Even though naysayers have argued against the possibility since at least the 1950s, many today believe Indian Rock marks a sacred Native American site. Granted, this line of reasoning might have originated with Mansfield, but as discussed previously, native relics, petroglyphs and burial mounds are known to have existed in the area. Discoveries are still happening, including a grain grinder located just a few miles away in Negley near Leslie's Run. Could the Painter's Knob carving mark a grave site as he suggests, or might it be meant as a warning? Roast some chestnuts on an open fire just in case, my friends, and feel the safety of modern times.

---

* Ohio Iroquois are often called Mingo, which is derivative of the Algonquin word *mingwe* meaning someone who speaks an Iroquoian language.

# CONCLUSIONS OF A GRAND EXPERIMENT

Interested in what sociological ripples would propagate from the resurrection of Barbara Davidson's nearly forgotten story, my father aptly deemed the Lion's Club Haunted Barn attraction "A Grand Experiment." The Pig Lady Facebook page continues to receive requests for information years after the fundraiser ended, as well as new paranormal encounter stories. It's a curious question of the chicken or the egg. Throughout the decades since the story of Barbara Davidson and other Little Beaver legends were first told, their popularity waxes and wanes, but with each peak, more encounters occur. More personal stories are revealed. Are ghosts real, or are they a manifestation of cerebral impulses derived from fear? I don't have the evidence or qualifications to make a credible judgment, but I can say unequivocally that the role of ghost stories in folklore isn't going anywhere.

Ira Mansfield loved his campfire legends and feared the tradition was fading. In 1916, when the popularity of the spiritualism movement was in sharp decline, Mansfield wrote, "One hundred years ago when Rev. Hughes opened Greersburg Academy at Darlington, one of the pioneer settlers John Bridgeman* prophesied the school would educate out all belief in ghosts, and in a short time Mrs. Cory, an old neighbor dame of 97 years of age, remarked in tones of sadness: 'Ghosts are getting thin.'"[128] Lucky for us, his concern was unwarranted. Mansfield's stories have endured modification and short periods of obscurity in the nearly hundred years since his passing,

---

*John Bridgeman was the first tenant of John Hughes and a neighbor of Barbara Davidson according to Ira Mansfield's Pennsylvania Abstracts essay referenced earlier.

but they remain. Today's information age, which permits me to scour thousands of records with ease for evidence inferring the origins of these beloved tales from my home office, also propagates and popularizes the stories at a rate Mansfield couldn't hope to imagine.

The notion that intelligence tradecraft can be used to analyze folklore is intrinsically arbitrary considering the intentional inaccuracies incorporated in the formation of urban myth. Couple this with the reality that endeavoring to prove evidence meant to be fantastic is a puerile venture, and it's easy to dismiss results, but I treasured every minute of it. This exercise provided a unique avenue of approach toward understanding local history that piqued my curiosity more than any project I've worked personally or professionally in years. I wish I could do this for a living. Assessing adversarial strategic military capability to destroy our way of life day in and day out can be taxing. This is fun.

I am a skeptic, but my intentions behind this research are not to disprove the supernatural. While ancillary evidence contrary to some of the story's paranormal origins is attainable through research, such as in the case of Gretchen's Lock, personal experiences are tricky to refute. Much like I cannot substantiate the existence of green to someone afflicted with color blindness, it is evident that it is not my place to argue what someone may or may not have experienced. Perceptions of one's environment are their reality. If you've observed something you can't explain, I'd love to hear about it and would happily do so without cynicism. Ghost stories are like documentaries; some educate, but all are meant to entertain. It's why Ira and Rich, both erudite men enthusiastic about bettering those around them, chose the medium as a tool in their efforts to preserve local folklore.

Mansfield was a member of the National Geographic Society, American Philosophical Society and Pennsylvania Historical Society. He was a Civil War veteran, a Pennsylvania state senator for many years, vice president of Beaver College (now Arcadia University) and president of the board of trustees of Darlington's Greersburgh Academy. I'm a super fan. Personally, I feel the Cannelton to Sprucevale strip of the North Country Trail should be renamed Robin Hood to honor his efforts in preserving both the natural

> **ALSO, IN 1916**
> *The Winchester Repeating Arms Company sold its last model 1873 rifle. Afterward, Sarah Winchester, an ardent spiritualist, held a séance in Boston during which a medium advised her to build a mansion for her and the spirits of those killed by Winchester rifles, resulting in the thirty-eight-year construction of the Winchester Mystery House.*

and American histories of the region. Oswald's contributions are nearly as significant. I wouldn't have been as enthralled by Ira Mansfield's storytelling if it weren't for Rich's revitalization and continuation of the Barbara Davidson story. They both found unique and stimulating ways to inspire interest in preserving our heritage, and for that, they should be revered. That being said, I have some theories of my own about these stories.

## Alternative Origin Theories

Alternative analysis is a mandated requirement of intelligence analysis after the recommendations of the 9/11 Commission. It's meant to ensure all courses of action are considered and to avoid similar cognitive traps that led to the Iraqi weapons of mass destruction assessments proven to be flawed. It provides decision-makers with information from both sides of the coin so that the influence of the analyst's own biases has less effect on policy or command decisions. If the supernatural is not the cause of these legends, then I submit these alternatives.

### *The Pig Lady*

Mansfield's telling of Barbara's story is only meant to be that and nothing more. He is careful to describe the ghostly narrative as a local legend on par with Little Gretchen Gill and Esther Hale. It appears, however, that since Mansfield was the first to immortalize Barbara's legend in print, then an argument could be made that he may have modified the story, and for a good reason. If parts of the story only lived on in oral tradition at the time, then gaps were more than likely filled with some conjecture. It's entirely possible that Barbara existed and her life succumbed to a dark ending.

With that in mind, children are curious creatures, especially in the days before digital distraction. It's reasonable to hypothesize that Mansfield adapted Barbara's story to warn the children of Cannelton to stay away from his incredibly dangerous mines. Evidently, it worked on at least one occasion well after his passing thanks to "good-ole uncle Norm." That in and of itself makes the story meaningful beyond its entertainment value. Maybe it is just a lucky happenstance. Perhaps it was an efficient design.

Collapsed mine in Cannelton.

## *Gretchen's Lock*

Gretchen's purported cause of death is uncommon in Ohio today, but it may have been the most prevalent disease in nineteenth-century America. Malaria still affects nearly half of earth's human population. According to the World Health Organization, in 2015 there were 296 million new cases of the mosquito-spread disease worldwide, causing approximately 731,000 deaths. It's well documented that the early Columbiana County populace was fearful of the illness they called swamp fever, and Sandy and Beaver Canal slack pools and reservoirs compounded the problem.[129] Locals held up construction of parts of the canal being built by E.H. Gill for this very reason. Might this fear have spawned Gretchen's legend? While the canal sat dormant during the panic of 1837, a story about the alleged death of the chief canal engineer's daughter as a result of this debilitating affliction would have been a useful propaganda tool for those opposed to the canal's construction after Gill resigned from the project.

## *Esther Hale (Hole)*

At the initiation of the women's rights movement in America, an influential female church leader and outspoken abolitionist would be threatening to some. The denigration of a strong female personality could easily be the motivation behind the forging of a new storyline for Esther, one that described her as being so weak-minded that she couldn't possibly recover from being left at the altar by a disinterested man. It's markedly notable that Ira Mansfield, a man who was a fervent proponent of women's suffrage and who venerated women schoolteachers, did not proliferate this version of the story.

## *Indian Rock*

The last alternative I'll indulge is the most difficult. The rest of the stories discussed, such as the Mushroom Lady, are probably designed purely to entertain, but Indian Rock is one I can't claim to understand. On the one hand, the U.S. government deemed it fit to declare the carvings as aboriginal. On the other, respected scholars question the validity of its native origin. I don't pretend to have the requisite academic qualifications to dismiss their opinions; however, because their conclusions lack both detail and credible sources and methods used to formulate logical argumentation, I feel justified in questioning their findings. Likewise, I realize my improvised assessment of each story is susceptible to apophenia, the tendency to attribute meaning to perceived connections or patterns between seemingly unrelated things. More specifically, my perception of Indian Rock could be a result of pareidolia, a type of apophenia involving the perception of images or sounds in random stimuli. Maybe it is just a birdbath very near another source of water, but my gut says no.

Arrowhead?

My most recent trip to the site had me questioning if it was a face at all. The rock lies on an almost perfect north–south line as if it were a directional marker. Could this be a coincidence? Probably, but it had me wondering if the "face" was actually the depiction of a notched arrowhead pointing at something important to whoever carved it. Perhaps the crude face was added later. In developing this theory, I freely admit that it undeniably could be influenced by the Indian Rock legend. As a tribute to both Rich and Ira, I'll leave it to you to decide the validity of this alternative.

# NOTES

## Introduction

1. Washington, *Journal*, http://digitalcommons.unl.edu/etas/ee.
2. Misencik, *George Washington*.
3. Ibid.
4. McCord, *History of Columbiana County*.

## Chapter 1

5. *Encyclopedia of Genealogy*.
6. Mansfield, *Historical Collections*.
7. *Biographical Sketches*.
8. Mansfield, *Historical Collections*.
9. Ibid.
10. Ibid.
11. Ibid.
12. Ibid.
13. Ibid.
14. Ibid.
15. Reader, *History of the Newspapers*.
16. Mansfield, *Ohio and Pennsylvania Reminiscences*.

## Chapter 2

17. White, *Supernatural Lore*.
18. Mansfield, *Historical Collections*.
19. White, *Supernatural Lore*.
20. Kellogg, *Frontier Retreat*.
21. Bausman, *History of Beaver County*.
22. Ibid.
23. Ibid.
24. Ibid.
25. White, *Supernatural Lore*; Kellogg, *Frontier Retreat*.
26. Bausman, *History of Beaver County*.
27. Mansfield, *Ohio and Pennsylvania Reminiscences*.
28. Ibid.
29. Mansfield, *Historical Collections*.
30. Mansfield, *Ohio and Pennsylvania Reminiscences*.
31. White, *Supernatural Lore*.
32. Richard and Henry, *History of Beaver County*.
33. Bausman, *History of Beaver County*.
34. Mansfield, *Historical Collections*.
35. Bausman, *History of Beaver County*.
36. Reader, *History of the Newspapers*.
37. Mansfield, *Historical Collections*.
38. Ibid.; Mansfield, *Ohio and Pennsylvania Reminiscences*.
39. Ibid.
40. Ibid.
41. Gowdy, *Marriages and Vital Records*.
42. Beaver County Register of Wills (n.d.), Probate Records, 1803–1917; Index to Register's Office, 1803-1965, retrieved from Ancestry.com.
43. Davidson, Revolutionary War Pension and Bounty Land Warrant Application File B. L. Wt. 1249-300, William Davidson, Penn. Retrieved from National Achieves Catalog, https://catalog.archives.gov.
44. Bausman, *History of Beaver County*.
45. Davidson, Revolutionary War Pension.
46. Ibid.
47. Mansfield, *Ohio and Pennsylvania Reminiscences*.
48. Archives and Records Administration, War of 1812 Service Records.
49. Ancestry, Federal Census, 1850, https://search.ancestry.com/search/db.aspx?dbid=8054.

50. Bausman, *History of Beaver County*.
51. Ibid.
52. Bricker, "George Foulkes."
53. Mansfield, *Historical Collections*.
54. Bausman, *History of Beaver County*.
55. Williams, *Orderly Book*.
56. Elbogen, "Violent Behavior."
57. White, *Supernatural Lore*.
58. L. Cranmer-Byng, *Buddhist Scriptures*.
59. O'Donnell, *Ghosts*.
60. Le Fanu, *Uncle Silas*.
61. Lake, *Weird Maryland*.
62. Scary for Kids, "Pig Lady."

## Chapter 3

63. Gard and Vodrey, *Sandy and Beaver Canal*.
64. Willis, Henderson and Coleman, *Weird Ohio*.
65. Burgess-Whitehill, *In Tune*.
66. Woodyard, *Haunted Ohio II*.
67. Haughton, *Lore of the Ghost*.
68. Mansfield, *Historical Collections*.
69. Mansfield, *Ohio and Pennsylvania Reminiscences*.
70. Mansfield, *Historical Collections*.
71. Fuller, *History of the Upper Ohio Valley*.
72. Ensign, *History of Columbiana*.
73. Rice, *History of the Hole Family*.
74. E. Lewis, (1850). First Month (Died), *Friends Review; Religious Literary and Miscellaneous Journal*.
75. Rice, *History of the Hole Family*.
76. Rice, *History of the Hanna Family*.
77. Gard and Vodrey, *Sandy and Beaver Canal*; Rice, *History of the Hanna Family*.
78. Ibid.
79. Ibid.

## Chapter 4

80. Mansfield, *Historical Collections*.
81. Ibid.
82. Gard and Vodrey Jr., *Sandy and Beaver Canal*.
83. Willis, Henderson and Coleman, *Weird Ohio*.
84. Gard and Vodrey Jr., *Sandy and Beaver Canal*.
85. Ibid.
86. Dunaway, *History of the James River*.
87. Creigh, *History of the Knights Templar*.
88. Directors, *Proceedings of the Stockholders*.
89. Minor, "Canal Chronology."
90. Strickland, Gill and Campbell, *Reports, Specifications and Estimates*.

## Chapter 5

91. Willis, Henderson and Coleman, *Weird Ohio*.
92. Dead Ohio, "Beaver Creek (Sprucevale Ghost Town)," http://www.deadohio.com/beavercreek.htm.
93. Willis, *Big Book*.
94. *Time*, "CRIME: Floyd Flushed," October 22, 1934.
95. Vivanio, "Ghost Boasts," *Vindicator*, November 1, 2003.
96. Father John A. Leger, obituary, *Pittsburgh Press*, February 4, 1955.
97. Haughton, *Lore of the Ghost*.
98. Ibid.

## Chapter 6

99. Mansfield, *Ohio and Pennsylvania Reminiscences*.
100. Fout, *Dark Days*.
101. Mansfield, *Historical Collections*.
102. Ibid.
103. Ibid.
104. Ibid.
105. McCord, *History of Columbiana County*.
106. Williams, *Orderly Book*.
107. Mansfield, *Ohio and Pennsylvania Reminiscences*.

108. Ibid.
109. Mansfield, *Historical Collections*.
110. Misencik, *George Washington*.
111. Mills, *Archaeological Atlas*.
112. Duafala, "Ira F. Mansfield."
113. Mansfield, *Ohio and Pennsylvania Reminiscences*.
114. Bausman, *History of Beaver County*.
115. Philbrick, *Mayflower*.
116. Mansfield, *Historical Collections*.
117. Ibid.
118. Ibid.
119. U.S. Bureau of Recreation, *Little Beaver Creek*.
120. Murphy, "Cannelton 'Sun God'."
121. Ibid.
122. Swauger, "Further on the Cannelton 'Sun God.'"
123. Bauder, "Face of Mystery."
124. Mansfield, *Ohio and Pennsylvania Reminiscences*.
125. Smith, "'Sun God' Rock."
126. Fuller, *History of the Upper Ohio Valley*.
127. Johnson, *Legends, Traditions*.

## *Conclusions*

128. Mansfield, *Historical Collections*.
129. Gard and Vodrey, *Sandy and Beaver Canal*.

# BIBLIOGRAPHY

Ancestry. U.S. Federal Census, 1850. Census Place: Darlington, Beaver, Pennsylvania; Roll: M432_750; Page: 119B; Image: 239. https://search.ancestry.com/search/db.aspx?dbid=8054.
Archives and Records Administration. U.S., War of 1812 Service Records, 1812–1815. Retrieved from National Archives and Records Administration. Index to the Compiled Military Service Records for the Volunteer Soldiers Who Served During the War of 1812.
Bauder, B. "The Face of Mystery: Legends Abound but Rock Carving's Origin Is Unknown." *Beaver County Times*, September 14, 1998.
Bausman, J.H. *The History of Beaver County and Its Centennial Celebration*. Vol. 2. New York: Knickerbocker Press, 1904.
*Biographical Sketches of Leading Citizens of Beaver County Pennsylvania*. Buffalo, NY: Biographical Publishing Corporation, 1899.
Bricker, D.D. "George Foulkes: The Story of an Unsung Legend." Varsity Tutors. www.varsitytutors.com/earlyamerica/early-america-review/volume-4/george-foulkes-the-story-of-an-unsung-legend.
Burgess-Whitehill, A.A. *In Tune with Spirits*. Hookstown, PA: Stitches and Strings Publications, 2002.
Campbell, T. "Stranger than Fiction: The Real Blair Witch Haunting that New Horror Film Is Based On." *Sun*, September 24, 2016.
Cartwright, R. *Gretchen's Wood*. N.p.: H'chtelegoth Press, 2014.
Clark, E.L. *A Record of the Inscriptions on the Tablets and Gravestones in the Burial Grounds of Christ Church, Philadelphia*. Philadelphia: Collins Printer, 1864.
Creigh, A. *History of the Knights Templar of the State of Pennsylvania*. Philadelphia: J.B. Lippincott & Co, 1868.
"CRIME: Floyd Flushed." *Time*. October 22, 1934.

# BIBLIOGRAPHY

Cusick, D. *Sketches of Ancient History of the Six Nations.* Tuscarora Village, NY: Cooley & Lathrop, 1828.

Darlington, M.C. *History of Colonel Henry Bouquet and the Western Frontiers of Pennsylvania, 1747–1764.* Pittsburgh: Privately printed, 1920.

Davidson, J.A. (n.d.). Revolutionary War Pension and Bounty Land Warrant Application File B. L. Wt. 1249-300, William Davidson, Penn. Retrieved from National Achieves Catalog: https://catalog.archives.gov.

Dead Ohio. "Beaver Creek (Sprucevale Ghost Town)." www.deadohio.com/beavercreek.htm.

Debartolo-Carmack, S. *Your Guide to Cemetery Research.* Cincinnati, OH: Betterway Books, 2002.

Directors, P.A. (1837–1864). *Proceedings of the Stockholders in the Richmond and Petersburg Rail Road Company, at Their General Meetings: and Reports Made by the President and Directors to the Stockholders.* Richmond, VA: T.W. White.

Duafala, A.P. "Ira F. Mansfield: A Man of Industry, A Man of Nature." *Milestones (The Journal of Beaver County History)* 38 (n.d.).

Dunaway, W.F. *History of the James River and Kanawha Company.* New York: Columbia University, 1922.

Elbogen, E.B. "Violent Behavior and Post-Traumatic Stress Disorder in U.S. Iraq and Afghanistan Veterans." *British Journal of Psychiatry* (2014): 368–375.

*Encyclopedia of Genealogy and Biography of the State of Pennsylvania.* New York: Lewis Publishing Co., 1904.

Ensign, D.W. *History of Columbiana County Ohio.* Philadelphia: J.D. Lippincott and Co., 1879.

Fout, F.W. *The Dark Days of the Civil War.* N.p.: F.A. Wagenfuehr, 1905.

Fuller, B.A. *History of the Upper Ohio Valley.* Vol. 1. Madison, WI: Democrat Printing Company, 1891.

Gard, R., and W.H. Vodrey Jr. *The Sandy and Beaver Canal.* East Liverpool, OH: John Taylor, Printer, 1952.

Gowdy, C.L. *Marriages and Vital Records of Western Pennsylvania and Eastern Ohio (1820–1868).* Apollo, PA: Closson Press, 1996.

Haughton, B. *Lore of the Ghost.* Franklin, NJ: Career Press, 2009.

Hintzen, W. *The Border Wars of the Upper Ohio Valley (1769–1794).* Manchester, CT: Precision Shooting, 2001.

Johnson, E. *Legends, Traditions, and Laws of the Iroquois, or Six Nations and History of the Tuscarora Indians.* Lockport, NY: Union Printing and Publishing Company, 1891.

# BIBLIOGRAPHY

Jordan, J.W. *Encyclopedia of Pennsylvania Biography*. Vol. 1. New York: Lewis Historical Publishing Company, 1914.

Kellogg, L.P. *Frontier Retreat on the Upper Ohio, 1799–1791*. Madison, WI: Cantwell Printing Company, 1917.

Lake, M.M. *Weird Maryland: Your Travel Guide to Maryland's Local Legends and Best Kept Secrets*. New York: Sterling Publishing Co., 2006.

L. Cranmer-Byng, D.S. *Buddhist Scriptures*. London: John Murray, 1913.

Le Fanu, J.S. *Uncle Silas: A Tale of Bartram-Haugh*. London: Richard Bentley, 1864.

Lewis, E. (1850). First Month (Died). *Friends Review; Religious Literary and Miscellaneous Journal*.

Mansfield, I.F. *Historical Collections: Little Beaver River Valleys*. Beaver Falls, PA: Tribune Printing Company, 1914.

———. *Ohio and Pennsylvania Reminiscences*. Beaver Falls, PA: Tribune Printing Company, 1916.

McCord, W.B. *History of Columbiana County and Representative Citizens*. Chicago: Biographical Publishing Company, 1905.

Mills, W.C. *Archaeological Atlas of Ohio*. Columbus, OH: Fred J. Heer, 1914.

Minor, D. (2005). "A Canal Chronology." Eagles Byte Historical Research. http://home.eznet.net/~dminor/Canals.html.

Misencik, P.R. *George Washington and the Half-King Chief Tanacharison*. Jefferson, NC: McFarland & Company Inc., 2014.

Murphy, J. L. "The Cannelton 'Sun God.'" *Pennsylvania Archeologist* (1978): 16–19.

Obituary, Father John A. Leger. *Pittsburgh Press*, February 4, 1955.

O'Donnell, E. *Ghosts, Helpful and Harmful*. London: William Ryder & Son, 1924.

Parsons, E. *The Life of George Washington, First President of the United States, 1789–1797*. Chicago: Laird & Lee, 1913.

Philbrick, N. *Mayflower: A Story of Courage, Community, and War*. New York: Penguin Group, 2006.

Reader, F.S. *History of the Newspapers of Beaver County, Pennsylvania*. New Brighton, PA: F.S. Reader and Son, 1905.

Register of Wills, B.C. (n.d.). Probate Records, 1803–1917; Index to Register's Office, 1803–1965. Retrieved from Ancestry.com.

Rice, C.E. *A History of the Hanna Family*. Alliance, OH: Aden Pim & Son, Printers, 1905.

———. *A History of the Hole Family in England and America*. Alliance, OH:

# BIBLIOGRAPHY

R.M. Scranton Publishing Co., 1904.

Richard, J.F. and T. Henry. *History of Beaver County, Pennsylvania*. Philadelphia & Chicago: A. Warner and Company, 1888.

Scary for Kids. "Pig Lady" August 11, 2014. www.scaryforkids.com/pig-lady.

Smith, H. "'Sun God' Rock and Johnny Appleseed." September 9, 2014. http://helenesmith1.blogspot.com/2014/09/sun-god-rock-and-johnny-appleseed.html.

Strickland, W., E.H. Gill and H.R. Campbell. *Reports, Specifications and Estimates of Public Works in the United States of America*. London: John Weale, 1841.

Swauger, J.L. "Further on the Cannelton 'Sun God.'" *Pennsylvania Archeologist* (1990): 88–89.

Timbs, J. *The Romance of London: Supernatural Stories, Sights and Shows, Strange Adventures and Remarkable Persons*. New York and London: Ballantyne Press, 1868.

U.S. Bureau of Recreation. *Little Beaver Creek, Ohio and Pennsylvania: Wild and Scenic River Study*. Washington D.C.: U.S. Government Printing Office, 1975.

Vivanio, J. "Ghost Boasts." *Vindicator*, November 1, 2003.

Walton, D. *Rivers of Destiny*. Koppel, PA: Beaver County Historical Research and Landmarks Association, 199.

Washington, G. a. (1754). *The Journal of Major George Washington* (1754). digitalcommons.unl.edu/cgi/viewcontent.cgi?article=1033&context=etas.

White, K. "Family Ties—Genealogy Project Leads to Forgotten Burial Site." *Morning Journal News*, July 12, 2015.

White, T. *Supernatural Lore of Pennsylvania: Ghosts, Monsters and Miracles*. Charleston, SC: The History Press, 2014.

Williams, E.G. *The Orderly Book of Colonel Henry Bouquet's Expedition against the Ohio Indians, 1764*. Pittsburgh: Mayer Press, 1960.

Willis, J.A. *The Big Book of Ohio Ghost Stories*. Mechanicsburg, PA: Stackpole Books, 2013.

Willis, J.A., A. Henderson and L. Coleman. *Weird Ohio*. New York: Sterling Publishing Co. Inc., 2005.

Winterburn, G. *Scenes of Little Beaver Creek*. Self-published, 1992.

Woodyard, C. *Haunted Ohio II: More Ghostly Tales from the Buckeye State*. Dayton, OH: Kestrel Publications, 1992.

# ABOUT THE AUTHOR

Michael Kishbucher resides in Virginia with his lovely wife and daughters but grew up in both Cannelton, Pennsylvania, and Negley, Ohio. In his spare time, Mike writes and volunteers, working stewardship and citizen science projects as a certified Virginia Master Naturalist. He is a member of the Little Beaver Historic Society, the International Society for Contemporary Legend Research and thoroughly enjoys "free-searching" for a certain astonishing podcast. Michael first learned intelligence tradecraft while serving in the U.S. Air Force, rising from the enlisted ranks to retire as a field grade officer. Michael earned a Master of Science in Strategic Intelligence degree from the Defense Department's National Intelligence University. For the past twelve years, Michael has analyzed adversarial military capability for the Defense Intelligence Agency as a civilian in federal service. He doesn't believe in ghosts (yet), and he thinks it's bizarre that authors always write this particular section of books in the third person.

*Visit us at*
www.historypress.com